# understanding thursday

## brett alan coker

(Original Cover)

**understanding thursday**

Brett Alan Coker

# A
# T.uesday's L.ife B.ooks
## *inspiration*

---------------------------------------

<u>Series One - Book Two of Nine</u>
### understanding thursday
*( - November 14<sup>th</sup>, 2001 - September 15<sup>th</sup>, 2003 - )*

Original Cover Photo - Brett Alan Coker
Back Photo - Shala Anne Owen

© 2003 Brett Alan Coker
ISBN 979-8-89379-379-6

## ... dedications ...

for Jonah Matranga from Onelinedrawing - for being a hell of a great guy

for Geoff Rickly from Thursday - one of the greatest poet/lyricists since Ian Curtis

for Kris Roe from The Ataris - for buying me a jack n' coke, sending me a christmas card, and making Elliott's birthday incredible

for Andrew McMahon from Something Corporate - for writing "Globes & Maps", "Me & the Moon" and "Konstantine." who majored in sweet-ass rock (with an emphasis in set-list creation)

for Matt Embree from the Rx Bandits - for taking the time to speak to those who will listen, making statements without preaching, and not talking down to an audience

for Christopher Ender Carrabba from Dashboard Confessional - for paving the way for us guys who don't play sports, or drive fast cars, and aren't afraid of their emotions

for Timothy Lee Bonnette Jr. the author of The Tale of Digby - for being a great confidant and a major influence on me. you have taught me a lot. you surprise me everyday

for the greats who inspired me: Hubert Selby Jr., Henry Rollins, Jim Carroll, Jack Kerouac, Allen Ginsberg, William S. Burroughs, Ian Curtis, Chuck Palahniuk, Shel Silverstein, Stephan Chbosky, Robert Smith, Jeffrey Eugenides

and to my friends, old and new:
Kirk•, Luke•, Derek•, Aaralyn•, Caroline•, Eric, Amber•, Elliott•, K.R.•, Ariana•, Loni•, Julie•, Tucker•, Roger•, Jon, Mr. Flynn•, Mr. Quint•, Lance•, Ainsley• ...

... Will• and Marilyn• ...

without you i would only have half a book.
hopefully the day will come where the past doesn't matter.

... and to Kelly ...

... who is only comparable to the stars themselves.

... endorsements ...

### .books.

The Perks of Being a Wallflower, Diary, Choke, Survivor, The Basketball Diaries, Forced Entries: The Downtown Diaries, On the Road, The Catcher in the Rye, The Great Gatsby, Junky, Requiem for a Dream, The Fall of America, Howl and other Poems, The Boys on the Tracks, Devil's Knot: the True Story of the West Memphis Three, The Tale of Digby, Middlesex, The Virgin Suicides, The Room, Last Exit to Brooklyn, The Moon is Down, A Clockwork Orange, The Wanting Seed, Cry the Beloved Country, Touching From a Distance, Lullaby, Black Coffee Blues, Life of Pi, Ishmael, The Sign and the Seal

### .films.

Day for Night, The 400 Blows, The Mosquito Coast, Magnolia, Requiem for a Dream, Halloween, Salò, The Hidden Fortress, The Crow, Leon: The Professional, The Goonies, The Monster Squad, Marat/Sade, Suspiria, Phenomena, Juliet of the Spirits, 8 1/2, Amarcord, Brazil, 12 Monkeys, Pi, Chasing Amy

### .bands.

Something Corporate, Rx Bandits, Onelinedrawing, The Ataris, Further Seems Forever, The Juliana Theory, Yellowcard, The All-American Rejects, Authority Zero, Sigur Rós, Dashboard Confessional, Steel Train, The Early November, Atreyu, Elliott Smith, Piebald, Thursday, Sparta, Jimmy Eat World, Finch, Ben Folds, The Get Up Kids, Autopilot Off, Stewart, Brand New, Good Charlotte, The Movielife, New Found Glory, Dreamer, Statistics, Codeseven, Sugarcult, Rufio, A.F.I., Fenix Tx, The Starting Line, The Used, Twothirtyeight, Fairweather, Anything But Joey, Joy Division, The Cure, Smashing Pumpkins, Radiohead, Sublime, Beethoven, John Coltrane, Miles Davis, Bone Thugs-N-Harmony, Snoop Dogg, Armor For Sleep, Abandoned Pools, Anberlin, Celebrity, Acceptance, Elliott, Coheed & Cambria, Mogwai, Explosions In The Sky

## ... introduction ...

i began this book of poetry very simply but scared. i wasn't sure where it would take me or if i would be able to fill another book. with 'til the streetlights came on i had no time frame, no real beginning, and no real end. i had dozens and dozens of poems that i had written in different styles in various notebooks in myriad places; there was no true chronology or linear structure. i just took what i had and fit them in the best order i could come up with. it was november of 2001 and i had been carrying around the same little sketch-book-turned-book-of-poetry, with no great output and no set schedule to write. so i figured it was time to start a new section of life. just a month before, a two-year-long relationship had ended so it seemed to be the perfect time for new beginnings. i slapped all of the 'til the streetlights came on pieces together and put them on the shelf. i then picked up a new sketch book, turned it into a new book of poetry and set off to see where it would lead. i said then that what i needed was an end. just like a fortune cookie i would get later in life which read: always begin with an end in mind. so i decided that once i fill this "little black book with my poems in it" (Pink Floyd reference) then this book will be done. so 300 blank pages were filled over a period of almost two years and the result is what lies ahead of you.

i have always considered myself an extremely stylized person and by that i mean slightly neurotic. everything i do must be done the same way. with 'til the streetlights came on every piece had to be complete, there were no fragments. and each poem had to have a title. with understanding thursday i shattered that strict form as much as i honored it. around the same time i began this book i also began to name the pens i use. i have carried a pen in my pocket for many years and i began to give each one a name and a life. i set myself rules of usage for my pens. i could only write in my book of poetry and my journals with my present pen. and once that pen ran out of ink i would then retire it and move on to a new pen. i would buy these three packs of papermate flexigrips that come with a purple, green, and gray pen. and that was the order i would use them. purple first because i hate purple, then green and then gray. through the course of this book i have retired nineteen pens. that is just about one pen per month. and in that time period i only misplaced one pen and had to replace him with a clone. those pens in order of usage are: bob, betsy, spike shinizzle, plum crazy, sprite, muted demon, tripsy, sublime, broken angel, vera lynn, exodus, k.h.b.s.w.t.g., splurge, digby, outsider, change, flyboy, dagger 2.0, and konstantine.

so here i am all crazed and neurotic, following these strange rituals and practices, yet i also blow apart many rules i set forth previously. in understanding thursday i have broken away from always completing my pieces. there are many small fragments and many of these are left untitled.  they are only given distinction by the dates on which they were written.  i also tried very hard to keep a tight schedule on a piece.  usually i would not begin a new poem until ending the one i was currently working on.  that too was not the case with this book, i would write a few lines one day and then return to it many months later.  i always felt that this was wrong because poems should be written in the moment, and if you let them go unfinished for too long then the poem changes from its original theme.  i found this was actually to my advantage and was quite surprised how well some of these pieces turned out.

another thing i must mention is that in the latter part of the book you may find a few lines repeated from poems in the first half of the book.  this does not happen too often but i was afraid if i did not explain why i would come under ridicule.  much like in my early works in 'til the streetlights came on i spent a lot of time with rhyme schemes and all of that junk.  i would soon drop that all together and eventually grow to despise rhyming poetry.  but something in me slowly made me go back to that form.  i began to write pieces with the mindset that they would be used as lyrics for songs, some of which have been put to music and function quite well.  in writing some song lyrics i began to reuse phrases i really liked from my writings.  all poems that were initiated as song lyrics will be labeled (song), this will tell you that they may contain lines stolen from other poems.

and finally the last thing i would like to talk about is the titles of my poems.  i have always attempted to stay away from obvious titles.  for example in 'til the streetlights came on there is a piece called "no difference."  we had to write this as an assignment.  the assignment was to write about hands.  and as you may have noticed i did not call it "hands" nor did i even use the word "hands" in the piece at all.  in understanding thursday i followed through on this as best i could to have titles that were very obscure and for the most part had nothing to do with the poem, and if they did it was some sort of hidden meaning.  one thing i am extremely proud of with this book is that unlike 'til the streetlights came on (where every other title was stolen from another place) most of the titles here are of my own creation.  i changed from stealing stuff from other people's works and began to use my own inside jokes and creations.  still a few titles are homages to other works and the only reason for that is because in some roundabout way they relate to the poem, and if you look close enough you may figure out how.

• after a name indicates that it has been changed.
\* after a title indicates it is lifted from another source.

In order to conserve space and keep these books as inexpensive as possible I have allowed - when applicable - for multiple complete poems to be on a single page.

**understanding thursday**

## jungle finger

a year i have been here
lying on the grass
tears watering the land
beneath my aching head
he is down there
only feet below
i pray someday we can reach one another

i miss the smile on his face
the warmth of his heart
it is not fair that these things happen
he is down there
only feet below me
never will he speak
never will he laugh, or cry

i think of all the things we saw
things we did and wish we had not
things we will never do
was the time we had enough
to fill my heart so full
that i will never forget these things?
i'll find out someday
six feet above him
always by his side

## _____ can't wait 'til next tuesday

other places all around me
other towns, cities, states
other countries and people
and i feel so left out
i am a loner in a world of corporations
a single leaf on a bare tree
i drive in front of the line
i turn left, only to see
the others behind me go right

i fly against the flock of birds
i get last year's hot toy
last season's hot shirt
the hot band's last album
last year's model of car
receiving leftovers of leftovers
hand-me-downs from someone
who never wanted the stuff
        in the first place

i write when others want to hear me
i speak when they want to talk
i ask questions when they want answers
i touch when they want space

when they wanna fuck i wanna sleep
when i want them
they want another
she wants me
when i want someone else
i want her
after she already left

i am tired of being the one
driving south on a northbound lane
wearing jeans in the summer
long hair when others have short
short when they have long
one step behind the crowd
laughing at a punchline
when they are saddened by a sorrowful tale
giving my condolences before there is even a corpse

all of these places, these worlds
feel as if they are here to fuck with my mind
to tear at my flesh and burn my heart
even more than i do

i am a floor to be shat upon
and used as their stomping ground
helping them attain riches and glory
using my hard earned cash
and constantly fading time

i am the drain of the world
       clogged with the waste
             of yesterday

### crazy diamond *

... goes round and round.

cross paths that were never known
known of paths never crossed
followed as close a trail i could
so many choices so many ways

what would it be like if i never ventured out?
only gave into the thoughts deep inside my soul
telling me that no matter what i do
happiness will never be had
love will never be found
the demons in my mind of mistakes in my past

eat through my power
showing me that i'll never be a winner
how can i fight them any longer?
the demons are my thoughts, my anxiety
my inhibitions, and fear
worrying about them, i give birth to more
they all tear me to pieces
saying i can never shine
never be bright
never ever be free
so i give in to the darkness
i feel i must

there are ups and downs
and leaps and bounds
yet it all ...

## corey's horse

topeka born
lenexa raised

feet scorching from asphalt suburbia
jeans stained green with kansas grass

living on the edge of civilization
slowly moving in, being pushed in
surrounded and overtaken by new blood
new homes, and lives
the whole world to me is backyards
as i grow it will be more
still only a radius of five miles
i have become comfortably numb
      with my dying childhood
every time i cry, parts of me dissolve
every time i bleed, the kid dies more
the kid in my bones and marrow
the one i love and miss so much

i watch old things shrink
a tree i used to climb
a dog i would ride
my bike and a trail i would travel
the desks i sat in
the blue plastic chairs
slowly one by one they fade away
eventually i will forget these things
not care about these things
not want to either

try to ignore change by ignoring what you were
      what you had
realizing your world is gone
your childhood is dead
your playground is rebuilt for a new generation
one that's better than you
your dreams killed to brew hope for others

i collect items, keepsakes
small tokens of my history
the more i mature

the more i want to destroy these things
they laugh at me and tease my senses
telling me to go back, go back
i want to burn my memories
grade cards and art projects
achievements from days gone by
a time only reachable in dreams
i cannot destroy them
they are all i have except for memory
two-dimensional reminders
        of a three-dimensional time

pictures only capture 1/24 of a second
they don't capture the thoughts
emotions, the tastes and scents
they do not capture your dreams and hopes
        nor will they ever
this is your life
        slowly ending
look back if you will
it will only kill you faster inside
        but slower out

you may still breathe and kick
however you only breathe to sigh at what you lost
kick to hurt yourself for the torture
you bring on

topeka born
lenexa raised
a true-blood kansan
with his heart fenced in

## fast food high school

have a seat, have a seat
read a book, read a book
turn it in, turn it in
go to lunch, go to lunch
eat a sandwich, eat a sandwich
be quiet, sit back down
listen, don't talk
move along, don't think
do this assignment, read this story
    next?
would you like to super-size that?
    any questions?
what do you mean you don't understand?
    any questions?
don't question me
leave me alone i'm arranging the dance
do busy-work i have to think about the game
    any questions?
have a seat, turn it in
go to lunch, eat a sandwich
fuck a cheerleader, wreck your car
push a nerd boy, deflower a princess
be quiet, sit back down
don't talk, listen
move along
you've graduated

## sage before beauty

kacey? hey kacey?
can you hear me calling?
calling you from the chilling night?
my arms are open and ready to warm you?
kacey do you remember me?
did you ever get naked and play your bongos?
do you still wear your homemade catwoman shirt?
i regret never knowing you
only your power as a writer
another contemporary like me

cichelli? hey cichelli?
can you hear me yelling?
yelling for you to run from the light?
it may burn your eyes
i often too get "lost in a day's life"
like you once wrote
"and i too must pass soon as death does loom"
we have not spoken in years
but some thoughts you scribed still stay in my mind
remember when we would joke
        in 2nd grade music class
just you, mindy and i?
time sure flies
when you don't have a clue where you are

valerie? hey valerie?
can you see me beckoning?
beckoning to watch the sunrise?
a bottle of rum and some reefer to make the day begin
you are a super pickle
and i feel for you at times
"to my sailor" was a masterous piece
yet sad, and that's no lie
now you are married and a world away
but hey
you have got a pen and paper, guess what?
so do i
let us start a new phase of our friendship
as the fiery sun comes up

shauna? hey shauna?
can you hear me asking?
asking for the time of day?
we have ten hours of daylight
let's see all we can, okay?
i wrote two poems about you, i never told you so
i recall you wrote one called
"the guy across the room"
i was the main subject, i'm still flattered
you still have not shared it though
i'm here if you ever need me

keith? hey keith?
can you hear me cheering?
cheering at the dying sun?
soon the darkness will cover all
and it is time for us to run
did you ever start your "nipple revolution"?
i said i'd lend a hand
ah fuck it, let's get stoned
pick our 'fros
and beat some nazi smurfs with rubber-bands

kassie? hey kassie?
can you see me smiling?
smiling at your face?
you were such a special lady
i fear no one told you so
i know you remember, 'cause i do
what i said that day in the hall
i meant it, still do
i'm glad it made a difference
if only for a day
i still have the note you gave me

alexandra? hey alexandra?
can you hear me laughing?
laughing at the fun we had?
talking and chatting in drama class
you said i was a good actor
i think you were just being polite
i was touched when you complemented my monologue
the one about brandon lee

i can still hear your voice
when you performed as ms. dickinson
        emily that is
i still have your critique sheet
of the piece i did from 'pulp fiction'
when i became christopher walken
do you ever think about me?

throughout my high school days
i was surrounded by such talent
such love and camaraderie
most of you mentioned i did not really know
nor have i seen you since
i miss you and it is depressing
that i never realized the masterful peers you were
until you've all gone away

## _____ **archive**

billy will you sing for me this night?
yell in that quivering voice
tell me about disarm tonight tonight
and end my infinite sadness
the world is a vampire, i know
except why do i thirst for blood?

emily will you read for me a poem tonight?
something dark that we can share my lady
i want to feel the coldness of your skin
as you read a sonnet about me
after i am dead we can finally be together

jon will you share your pain tonight?
fuel my rage with your lyrical sex
help me find a way out of my mind
hey daddy, tell me i am somebody someone
'cause i just wanna laugh again

roger will you mystify me tonight?
with songs about the worm
open your head so i can see inside
see if i can steal some tragic thoughts
power for my rise

edgar will you eulogize my dreams tonight?
as i sleep on the ground where you once laid
thinking of a raven and wanting it all to end
show me there is more to hate than pain
are there any benefits?

al will you show me how to court a young gal tonight?
sing her ballads that make her see me right
your music stays in my mind and soul
still, i'm tired of being alone
so, let's stay together, worlds apart

jim will you spot me a cap tonight?
my days have been hard and i need a fix
i want to stand beside you and yell
yell our spoken word from the tarry roofs of new york
sleep in a nod with me and let's

conquer the aberrations of night

hubert will you help me to fight my will tonight?
to not kill myself with wants and dreams
show me a way to deny my needs
let's stare at the sky and see the demons
slowly croon in the moonlight

james will you show me
your torment and despair tonight?
your art shows me some
but i want to hear some spoken word
do you dream of killing that drunk driver
that took your lover's life?
if i was you i would
i won't pretend, though, to know that pain

bruce will you spar me until i'm good tonight?
help me keep tone and fit so i can live long
        unfortunately unlike you
i saw brandon in a dream and he missed you
like the rest of us

brandon can you tell me about the beyond tonight?
prepare me for what lies ahead
if not i understand
you have already given me a lot
a hero and idol
i wish you were still here
        your father says "hi"

paul can you show me how to create life tonight?
so i can give birth to real feelings and emotions
tell the stories i must in a fashion that's right
if i could have the talent of anyone it would be you
but you deserve it more than me, it's yours

chuck will you be my mentor in cynicism tonight?
teach me textbook pessimism
and more of those useless facts
i hate being a narrow-minded consumer
that you are quick to judge and tear down
at least i am being degraded by the best

influences and idols and heroes of my past
i am all of you
i am who i am because of you

thank you

## survivor*

at times it is like i am a main course
something for someone to serve
      to another for consumption
to be thought about and prepared
there are rules of etiquette for my consumption
i am a fucking lobster
you crack my claws
then break my carapace
eat my meat with your three-pronged midget fork
you put me in a pot and slowly raise the temperature
so i die painlessly
but you don't cook me properly
you just toss me in the boiling water
and yell at me to be done quicker
eat me and enjoy
i'll eventually be your literal shit
i already feel like it so i could care less

## catwoman

kacey i saw you tonight
you saw me too
you recognized me yes
do you truly remember?
or am i, perhaps like many
        a nameless face from your past
i wanted to approach you, but did not
i wanted to touch you, but did not
i wanted to kiss you, but did not
i still want these things
it doesn't matter though
i'll never get them
that's fine i guess
when you saw me did you feel happy?
was it good to see me
        because you have thought of me too?
wondering what i have done with my life
did you ever think about me in high school?
what if? what could have been?
or was i just a friend to pass in the hall
        to forget tomorrow?
i'll never forget your voice, your style
the independence, the beauty
i wish i could say my longing was not all physical
some of it is, not all
i just want to know you
i am here

## guild

i am a fighting soldier
        on the battlefield of creation
i check the ink level in my pen
        like the bullets in a gun
i go into the world armed
        with only thoughts and unwritten word
a soldier can die but once
        i can die a million times and have
yet my glory will live forever

i've no real battle or war
        except to do what i was born to do
create tales and characters
        dictate my period of time
        and how it has affected me
i can be told my tales are filth
        unrealistic and surreal
that does not concern me
        what i create is unimportant
all that matters is the creating

i am a natural born storyteller
        fighting and dying in a land of repetition

       **for aaralyn • :**
orange n. 1. a semitropical evergreen tree of the genus citrus, with white flowers and round, yellowish-red edible fruit having a sectioned interior and sweet, acid juice. 2. a yellowish red.

eye n. 1. an organ of sight or of light sensitivity. 2. the faculty of seeing: vision. 3. a look: gaze. 4. the ability to perceive, judge, discriminate. 5. a point of vision. 6. something suggesting an eye <the eye of a needle> v. **eyed, eye·ing** or **eying.** to watch closely: look at. **-see eye to eye.** to be in complete agreement.

the combination of 1 part orange, and 2 parts eye results in a unique creation as dictated below:

       **bull?**
i saw her that night
time stood still
simple thoughts raced through my mind
all i could think about was beauty
looking at her i see this
wanting to feel close to her
allow her to be close to me
yet will it all work out?
she speaks like an angel
thinks pure and un-corrupt
unless she has been hiding her true self
everything inside tells me to pursue
should i? or see if she does first?
doubts overload my soul
am i good enough for her friendship?
       her trust?
years may pass before i earn either
and i am distraught
i know i cannot change my past
things i have done may
       and will affect her view of me
maybe she will see me striving to be a better man
years, once again, may pass before i can do so
how can i be able to make her my new friend?
our time together is short, i need to take that step
unless she takes it first
staring at me she tells me about herself

enchanted, i am, by her gorgeous eyes
only seeing her eyes as she speaks of the future
bathing in the amazing glow of her harvest eyes
and i hear every word
now she has made her move
        and told me of our friendship
getting nervous with these questions
        i have about us
ever being something more?
ever being something special?
yet something tells me
everything will come together
sadly, yet surely, this is my only chance
        to win her heart

## clockwork pupils

    for Aaralyn •

gazing at me
i look deep into them
    i know i can't lie or hide
their fiery hue will burn straight through
    all of my lies and excuses
treat her right, i tell myself
    and the warmth of her dazzling eyes
    will comfort you 'til dawn
looking long into her soul
    stroking her silky brunette hair
her long sensuous legs
    rubbing against mine
seeing in her
    hopefully, what she sees in me
the burning of my heart
    is at last a sanctuary
    for my hidden emotions
i have found someone special
    with sparkling lava eyes
the fresh orange gloss
    is delicious to the taste
the pleasant sweetness of her kiss
    the stunning tart of her lusting lips
a long night lies ahead
    a cold december night
to be kept warm with the passion
    of a beautiful gal with orange eyes

## prism attractions

plucking a string of a porcupine quill
strumming the mane of a flapper-esque lion
fingering the keys of a blind tiger
beating the hide of a rabid rhino
      cue up the playback
      and watch us collide

young pixies with jet-black eyes
snort back lines of crushed butterfly wings
starlet fairies inject in veins
the remains of unicorn horn
      nodding into a fantasy

pubescent warlocks striding into the stream
the three-eyed fish
      nibbling on sunken treasure
plankton covered mermaids
      devoured by molten dwarves
sucking on the marrow of skinless albinos
      who is next in line?
smoking the glow of fireflies
heartless angels
      strap on their gravity boots
step down upon fascist cherubs
      eating mammoth tusks
aries cuts down the forest
      a crab army's home
sea horses overtake neptune
      and his flounder harem

      oh to be

**_____nothing**

and i see these things
that i feel were meant for me
may not be up to the glory of my sufficiency
and i cry lovely tears of want
deep inside the child sobs
dreaming the pain of tomorrow
        this child was pure
          i made him so
now my rage has killed his heart
and i hide behind this false façade
why do i do these things?
why do i strive for all yet get nothing?
for centuries things will evolve
        change and recoil
        build up and boil
to a point of extreme falsity
fuck the nay-sayers of my generation
toiling with the structure of
        my narrowing resolve

## goth scribe

echoing through the ancient trees
       of wisdom and truth
blowing leaves whisper the secrets
       of an extinct society
            of philosophers and poets

branches crack and the silence is broken
nothing but the thoughts
       i think i am hearing
voices in my head spoken by
       dead people from my past

wading across the crystal stream
          the blackened swan and children dream
          becoming part of a general theme
frost thaws on shivering shrubs
       quivering with the trickles of love

pools of essence gather
       at the roots of a mystical stone foundation
       built merely for symbolism
a shrine to shine for years and months
       a day or two or not

and amidst this all is me
       a frozen boy with a voiceless scream

## a side in my thorn

certain things make me think
    of times when i made mistakes
wondering if i thought enough about it
    or perhaps not at all
these things i have done i am not proud of
    nor will i ever be
i have come so far and done so much
    so much i should not have
    and so much i should but didn't

is there ever going to be a middle ground?
where i do the things i should
and never do things i should not
    i doubt it too

all of the wrong things always feel so right
    at the time i mean
the right things do not always feel good
    not while in the moment
        years later it is felt and worth it

eventually my good will cancel out my bad
    maybe

i can dream at least

## more than what you allow
    for Marilyn •

so many times i felt content
simply touching your skin
the sweetness of your kiss
    the warmth of your hands
you made me feel like a man
you always had the power to see
    everything i felt inside
you knew when i was sad
    and when i made a mistake
i hurt you so much
    i still don't know why
always there whenever i needed you
    however i needed you
you were and are so much more
    than what i could ever need
unfortunately my want is too much
    and i commit these acts that kill
    your love and trust
i have tried and will try more
    to regain everything i have lost from you
    trust, love, friendship
    all equally important to me
"time will heal all wounds,
    but the reminder of a scar will stay."
these words are true
i know our love will blossom again
it will be magnificent
like you always have been
    and i strive to be

## just another teen

for the girl by the phone at ameristar casino, and saw 'not another teen movie' on december 28th, 2001 who was with a friend and wearing a blue coat

she is standing by the phone
she has been hurt
      her eyes tell me this
she is waiting for something, someone
      to come and save her from herself
men have only seen her for her body
never her truth, her inner beauty
she hates herself for falling in love
      too many times, for too little
putting too much of herself out
      to get too little back in return
she spends her days following, never leading
staying behind to hide her anguish
she can't show anybody who she really is
      for fear she will be too exposed
becoming a face in a crowd
crying at night alone, screaming in her mind
wanting that one honest man to comfort her
tell her "it will all be okay in the end."
      and hold her hand by the white picket fence
but for now she must still cower
her day will come, she knows this
she wants it oh so bad
and she will have it

yet today she is a broken angel
      in a realm of muted demons

**mason**

depleting sorrow
      an old man's pain
depleting regret
      an old man's trouble
depleting hope
      an old man's comfort
depleting knowledge
      an old man's tool
depleting dreams
      an old man's world
depleting life
      an old man's

## bourgeoisie

**v**
sins of the father
torment of the son
dread of the mother
anguish of the sister
at least it's a family thing

**vi**
kids in the city, kids in the streets
kids in the alleyways, kids on their feet
running from tomorrow
being hounded by today
chasing the tail of yesterday

**vii**
ticking away the time
the time of the antichrist
take a chance with redemption
but also risk damnation
just a roll of the dice

**viii**
blessed fools
righteous beasts
shoot the "h" between your feet
pop a pill and find a way
to enter your own salvation

## **prose soldier**

confusion of the masses
becomes the problem of the outsiders
inspection by the masses
becomes the problems of the outsiders
questioning by the masses
becomes the problems of the outsiders

answers from the outsiders
becomes comfort for the masses
advances by the outsiders
becomes ease for the masses
hard work and struggle by the outsiders
becomes relaxation for the masses

questioning by the masses of the outsiders
becomes persecution of the outsiders
the ones who make the world work and run
genocide of the outsiders by the masses
calms the minds and makes them feel secure
      for today
tomorrow they will realize they killed their motors
the outsiders are the motors
that run the mass machine

## millennial lamentation '02

the circle of life
        is a one-sided thing
in order for life to be great
        death has to be the patsy

a new year has been born
        and it is cherished and celebrated
last year died quickly with no one caring
        yet it gave us more than this year so far

they always say, "you can't know where you are going
        unless you know where you've been."
it seems like we don't care where we're going
        and hate where we've been
it feels like that to me

days go by and things can only change
will it eventually come full circle
        so i will become who i was five years ago?

god help me if that's true

_____ **your poem**
      for Cassie B.

i read the book your mother wrote
      and it made me feel for you even more
it showed that people go through a lot
      they change every day
      and learn from their mistakes
in a hundred years, no one
      truly, no one
      will ever understand
      what happened on that day
you were one of fifteen who left us
most people only care about thirteen of you
are you angry at eric and dylan too?
      like everyone else
or do you understand a little
      of their conflict and pain
nothing can ever make up to you, or anyone
      what they did for infamy
do you find it strange that in your book
      lyrics are quoted from a song by the band
      the whole catastrophe
      was supposedly because of?
you liked that band didn't you
do you see any connection between the two?
faithful people believe you said what you did
those who base what they believe on facts question it
i will never question if you said it or not
if you did that's for you and god to know
if you didn't, we all know you believe
what would you say to us
      and them if you had the chance?
would you clear up any questions about what you said
      or just let us believe what we want?

april 20th, 1999 - the day she said, "yes."

## free-nix

insider talk to me
i know you want and need to
insider are you sick of not being able to think?
is your job plastic-wrapped for you?
your religion sealed airtight?
relaxation not relaxing because of its safety features?

insider open up to me
i know you think, you are just afraid to speak
is your future carved in stone?
your dreams etched in biodegradable foam?
feel guilty for wanting to live your life for you
        instead of your kids?

insider cry on my shoulder
i know you're choking, it's okay for you to weep
angry that you put so much effort
        into four years of social interaction?
mad that you went to college
        for you parents and not you?
upset that your job is financially great
        but opposite of your dream?

insider make me proud
i know you can do it, take back your life
perhaps take that writing course for yourself?
buy that boat to fix it up?
write that novel that lives inside?
take your life back
it's never too late

## bourgeoisie

### ix
she cut his throat
and devoured his heart
drank his blood
and cried herself to sleep
wait, what?

### x
enter my wasteland
find all your gold
give up your mind
your body and your soul
the treasures of a childhood reborn

### xi
you never think
just do what they say
they know better, who are you?
what are you gonna do, try and be free?

### xii
roll the ball
take a chance
turn the knob
a leopard pants
i am slowly going crazy

## what most people would entitle "fight" but not me

fight the power
fight the pain
fight your parents
fight the cops
fight your teachers
fight your peers
fight your boss
fight the government
fight the media
fight society
fight your mind
fight the future
fight your past
fight your enemies
fuck, fight your friends
fight your thoughts
fight your morals
fight all ethics
fight dogma
fight your god
fight your devil
fight yourself
fight your idols
fight your heroes
fight your heirs
fight your leaders
fight your fans
fight your followers
fight
fight
fight
fuck it all
fight them all
fuck them all
fight it all
you only live once
waste it and fight

## bourgeoisie

### xiii
willie and the poor boys
bring your nickel
and unlock the past
secrets of the old days
ancient dogma released

### xiv
my wasteland is your home now
and nothing of you i ask
i hope i've made you happy
i've given all but my life
eventually i'll take that for myself

### xv
change your history
change your mind
change your appearance
change your thoughts
who wants to be unique?

### xvi
demon sauce
angel paste
jungle juice
desert love
commit me. please?

## _____ **bourgeoisie**

**xvii**
corey's horse died
before he could ever ride it
so now he
can't wait 'til next tuesday
something good might happen

**xviii**
he is coming
i wanna warn you
learn seven
it'll set you free
from the masterous epic

**xix**
i accepted the fact
that i am an outsider
i built my wall
i became the worm
defeating my mental demons
it'll all start again

**xx**
ten men
fourteen queens
fifty-one sons
sixty-eight fates
anyone seeing a pattern?

### elitist babies

plan their nights a week ahead
so everyone can be there
in a group they are all best friends
yet there are always inner circles
      to tease and backstab
      talk shit and negate
all is well when hidden in numbers
they don't have to bother with substance or feelings
      only about what to wear
they carouse and talk and converse
everything they say and do will be forgotten in days
they laugh and smile and hug and kiss
quietly deep inside they are always judging
re-accessing and computing in their minds
all is fun in numbers
when they go their separate ways
in jumps the pain, the depression
they know that they are truly alone
their friends are eye candy to slowly starve them
where did the love of the world go?
why did everybody go away?
where did i go wrong?
money can only buy things to be left behind
friendship is the only spiritual currency

## black knees
     for Eliza •

i opened it all up
    only to be shut down
there was something about you
    i loved but now hate

i gave you friendship
my heart, love, then body
you never gave me anything
    except three hours of lust

i held you only once
you cried in my arms
you needed someone
    and i was the only one you trusted

the last time i spoke to you in person
i needed to touch you
you refused to give me
    a single hug or any care

i listened when you needed it
i spoke when you allowed
everyday i thought would be the day
    we would finally give in to one another

that day never came
we were never more
we were only fake friends
    and useless lovers

i gave you my heart
when you only wanted my body
you gave me your body
when i wanted your love

it has been years since i've touched you
it has been years since i've seen you
it has been years since i've held you
but not more than days since i've thought of you

always still questioning
did i ever mean anything to you?
always still wondering
do you miss me too?

my whole being wants to hate you
wants to curse you
wants to forget you
yet why do i still love missing you?

i still can't believe
        what a lost child you were
i guided you the best i could
however i only guided you away from me

i wish i could say that you changed me
made me a better person
that our friendship was something true
i never lied to you so i won't start now

i only have two pictures of you
        and a dozen fading glimpses
a few worn-out phrases
a small tingle where you touched me

i cried for you once
and that was one time too many
it was 2 a.m. my first day of senior year
the day after you killed all hope

one thing i've always hated in life
is someone i know becoming someone i knew
you are no longer in my life like you were
not a day passes that i'm glad i never truly knew you

## in the parking lot at midnight
      for Chastity •

we were naked and touching
before we ever spoke as friends
you made me in your mind
      something that i'd never be
i made you out to be a piece of flesh
      to do everything i want
you put up with me
      and believed in us
why?
because you thought we'd grow to be more?
i wanted your body never your friendship or love
i used you and apologized then used you again
you fell for my lies and allowed it
why did i just now grow a heart
      years after i hurt you?

i can not begin to say all of the things i think
when your face floats around in my mind
i was your first kiss, your first touch
your first heartbreak
and i never cared about your feelings
you were such a special girl
and i never wanted to see that
i wasn't ready to deal with those kinds of emotions
i called you one day and told you
you still are what you may want to be
while i am a useless fuck
who deserves to be hurt tenfold
that still wouldn't be sufficient
when compared to your pain

i still think about you
about all of the mistakes i made
i'm sure you think of me too
for reasons unbeknownst to me
i'm sure you'd forget me if you could

now it's time to talk about "someday"

    someday we could meet again

someday we could want to start over
someday i could take you on a real date
someday i could treat you like a person
        learn about you
        ask you questions
        allow myself to see you as a friend
rewrite our penciled past with permanent ink
we could finally be what you couldn't have but wanted
we could finally be what i wanted too
        but wouldn't allow
i believe that things change with time
so people can grow to be better to the ones they hurt

## tuttle creek
for Mindy

floating on a raft with your friend in the river pond
    in the cool brown water
    on a warm summer day
i showed off and swam beneath you
for some reason i thought you were older than i
    shocked to find out you were younger

just like you i was camping
    with my family and friends
you kept trying to see us
    like my buds and i did you

do you remember that night on the trail?
when we had fifteen minutes alone
voices echoing from the darkness around us
    trees and bushes surrounding
the cool breeze of the midnight water

we held each other and kissed
we touched and you were nervous
    about exposing the scar on your chest
although i had seen it earlier
    when you were swimming
it didn't bother me then either
    still doesn't

do you remember finding our tent
    at 1 in the morning?
you and Angel watched 'Halloween' with us
    for about an hour
the following day do you recall?
you and i behind the run-down concession stand
    by the volleyball court and beach?

kissing again, touching
your body scented with that smell of the river
your shirt kind of damp
    from your bathing suit beneath
the smell of your wet hair

i remember kissing you, eyes open
memorizing every curve of your ear
feeling that mounting depression
knowing you'd disappear
i told you to remember me
        my name and my face
for someday i'll be famous
i'm still working on it

although short, our time was amazing
i will find you again
we may not be what we both remember
but it's nice to visit our memories
we were each other's for a day and a half
a piece of each other's past we remain
a part of our hearts still together

## _____justice

>for all of the ladies i have known

it is coming soon
the day i am confronted
>surrounded and attacked
i will cower in their circle
>yelling on my hands and knees
stripped of all of my faces
>that i use to hide
every girl, every woman
that i have ever known and touched
>will control me
they will devour me
they will yell
>"you are not who you think you are"
they will stone and kick me
>"you are not what you pretend to be"
they will kick and punch me
>"you like to think you are more than you are"
they punch and stab me
>"you act like you don't have feelings
>but you do"
they will stab me and pierce me with words
>"you told us you loved us
>then fucked us and left"
they will yell
>"you ruined our hearts
>and made it hard for us to love"
they will yell
>"you made us build a wall
>to hold out all real men"
everything i did and said to them
>has now become bullets
>in their emotional guns of thought
"you made us feel bad about ourselves"
"made us cry for your mistakes"
"made us weak"
"made us looked down upon
>in the eyes of our parents"
"laughed at by our friends"
you are all of the bad things
>our mothers warned us about

i will say, "i'm sorry"
then the curtain will rise and i will be center stage
    in the theatre of life
the world will see me weak and groveling
they'll laugh and cheer
    at my cowardice and begging
i will finally see that i do have feelings
yet i only care when it is myself being hurt
    too little too late

## porn star aristocracy

step into their world
and lose all self-control
give up individuality
hand over the keys to your freewill
and all of this makes me wanna
makes me wanna
wanna kill
but more importantly i wanna

they take your money in exchange for shit
feed you lies and make you sick
they take your lives and say you're weak
feed you bullshit and swear you're dumb
they strip you of power and give you rules
feed you answers that give you more questions
and all of this makes me wanna
makes me wanna
wanna kill
but above all i wanna
      fuck the bourgeois!
      fuck the bourgeois!

with their high-rise condos
or house in the hills
six-car garage and private-jet thrills
seven-figure salaries
barbie-doll figure wives
kings of industry pretending
rulers of the world façade
posh tight-ass daughters
their princess guise and debutante balls
versace wearing sons
viper, brothel and cocaine bills
living like fucking gods
killing freedom with trusts
taking lives and breaking families
only to make a few more bucks
and all of this makes me wanna
makes me wanna
wanna kill
and now also
      fuck the bourgeois!

        fuck the bourgeois!

they hide behind stolen money
fake friends, false enemies
shield themselves with titles and prestige
awards and medals and ribbons
things my bullets will still go through
promote themselves with bought media
golden crosses around their necks
million-plus churches in their neighborhoods
        forced million-plus churches in mine
all fronts to hide their raping and pillaging
whore buying and junk addictions
they use their religion-of-the-day
        to appeal to the no-man
but us no-man assholes are smarter than they think
we may not have the power
        the attorneys or the funds
only the lack of loss and care
        the killing mind and the guns
and all of this makes me wanna
makes me wanna
wanna kill
more than that i wanna
        fuck the bourgeois!
        fuck the bourgeois!

right in their silver-spoon sucking mouths
        and starbucks-latte-enema asses

all of the poverty stricken no-men yell
        fuck the bourgeois!
all of the white trash in the house yell
        fuck the bourgeois!
all of the future pedophiles and serial killers yell
        fuck the bourgeois!
all of the rebels in the house yell
        fuck the bourgeois!
all the outsiders in the house yell
        fuck the bourgeois!
fuck 'em 'til they bleed

        fuck the bourgeois!

## sewer rats

burning streets and muddied hearts
fuck goddamned pieces of fleshed martyrs
one time at the tower i saw my life,
    slowly being surrounded
        by things i don't understand
freezing gypsies and cum-dried men,
    on the streets of downtown, faceless tools
fuck the police and fuck people
    who say "fuck the police"
once i dreamed of The Farm
    surrounded by houses and subdivisions,
    block parties and barbecues
faceless tools with minivans and kids
killing the places i fucking love
at the place we call The Crossroads,
i never know which way to turn to go back in time
every way i take i always end up in my present
we used to play in a cistern
    and had a fort in a sewer in a place,
    we used to call 'hocker grove'
i no longer can crawl through the tunnel
    to go see my drawings of choker
    and the profanity on the walls
one time on a destination-less cruise to de soto
    we saw a lady who was
    driving a car that had one tire
completely worn away
    and was running on her rim
rainy days with fucking frogs
the whole existence of my mind slowly goes
    fuck i forget
we offered to help her and she was
    "drunk as fuck" to
    quote an overused phrase
she was looking for pflumm
    which was fifteen miles
    in the other direction
    she was in the wrong city
we changed her tire and she offered us weed
too young and naive to accept
fuck bitch, i'll take up that offer
    and toke it 'til dawn

             if you can draw me a map to
1987
with my 'He-Man' shit and soccer games
'Voltron' love and Alf's show
if i could bite the nose off of people i hate
i would eventually puke up a lot of noses
there was this place we called the racetrack
            for some unknown fucking reason
in the blue truck i'd risk tipping it
            by flying a hundred around an inclined curve
            "Through the Never" playing
i also used to fly up a street squeezing between cars parked on each
side blaring my horn
            at the scoggins' abode
fuck there is a useless talentless loser
            writing words right now
he used to follow his bus 117 home from school
            when he first began to drive
trying to show off and think he was cool
now i wish that the bus would've lead me back to 1991
gulf war time     vanilla ice       t-u-r-t-l-e power
met a good dude then
now called "jesticle" or "uncle jess" or "cudaboy"
fire bullets rubber or real at the police station on 87th
or at least put dishwashing liquid in the fountain
            like they did to the fountain on blackfish
hey piggies! i know who stole your computer
            for your radar machine
            you used to leave on residential streets
fuck off cause i won't tell you
stick a rusty nail in the sole of all who hate me
            they'll line up for miles
scalp all of those who i feared at some point
            they'll line up for miles
carve my initials on the foreheads of people who fucked with me
            and called me a "pussy"
            they'll be waiting for years
put a bullet in the brain of the person who let it all happen
            and spent his life trying to make it go away
in 1998 back at the tower
i held Mandy and we kissed in the cool breeze of night
eyes closed in the already surrounding darkness
two weeks later i became "unpure"

never regretted it
"who?" she'll say when asked about me
turmoil turmoil turmoil
hate me, okay, go ahead
fuck it's hard to love the past that you hate
want to redo the times you didn't enjoy
        all that much the first time
aimlessly wasting time and gas
        barreling through de soto's fields and
        gravel roads while skipping school
slaughter rockin'
loving that time so much
if i did it now it would simply be
        me trying to re-experience it
        as it feels now looking back on then
not experience it for the first time like i did then
not even thinking about now
fuck bonner springs police
        and the three guns pointed at my head
searching my truck
bad music playing from their patrol cars
hand coming out of the cuff
it would've been cool
        if they shot a hole through my neck
so i wouldn't have to taste the vomit
        escaping from my soul as i gave responses during their
interrogation
i used to touch and kiss this girl
        before we even knew what we were doing
she was one of my best friends
i've not seen her since 1991
        and she doesn't exist to me now
and i question if she ever did
kind of like my uncle that i've never met or seen
        nor knew existed until i was eight
it is so irresponsible that grievances
        and problems of yesterday affect
        people now who weren't even there
okay you have a problem with him but why can't i know him
        and give him a chance
fuck people in my past who tell me not to standout
fat-ass eskimos who have a fecal allergy
fuck me where do i come up with this shit?

if i'm ever committed
        they'll have no trouble proving my insanity
insanity bore and bred
        out of sane and rational decisions
in wamego at a sonic i saw this girl
        and fell in love with her
she dropped some change and said "fuck"
        and my mom and i thought it was funny
i never saw the girl again
faces people names places
all "dust in the wind"
yes, that's from kansas, much like my skinny ass

roger's emotions in melody and words
fuel my rage and need to block it all out
those looks that teachers gave me
those looks that authorities gave me
those looks that parents gave me
those looks that peers gave me
that "you're so worthless and stupid" look
fuck your bourgie sheep mouth
i am struggling, can you not see?
i struggle to see and to find what the fuck i am
who i've become, who i'll eventually be
oh yeah, variables
variables and objects, samples and little bitty tastes
all uniformly combined to make me
        unique and "original"?
made to be different yet told to fit in
whose idea is this?
can you feel me?
a slowly dying piece of composting shit?
why won't you touch me?
i eventually will find time to love
silly midgets with albino duck platters
dancing negro aristocrats lap dancing on my package
blonde-haired blue-eyed gals with m.s.
        massage my mushroom tip
washboard-stomached homos lick my ears
        and put twenties in my socks
no, it doesn't make sense to me either
it's all ramblings, blunt and pointless
internet sex, boy it's interesting

ass-cock licking, frog felching
penguin taint-rubbing, fish fisting
don't knock it 'til you try it
i met a midget once
        and got my picture taken with him
watched a movie with some guys from The Time
shook the hand of the star of 'H6'
        and fellow West alumni
let's just keep talking about me
on occasion i have a man-on-man love dream
        that makes me sick to my stomach
if you like that cool, that's fine
        it ain't my thing
sex on a roof while working
        try that on a warm summer night
'88 and hiding from car lights
        and throwing rocks from the shadows
fall off a slide sticky with late-night dew
fall to the ground and fuck your shoulder up
and stand crooked for years
pinty pinty bitty bitty bop bop
ice cream sodas with shasta black cherry
'Dream A Little Dream' and a living room fort
'The Goonies' every day eating yogurt
        and a bowl full of smarties
write a page of letters every day
        when not watching 'Duck Tales'
give codie a bath and pick up her shit with the appropriately named
"pooper scooper"
love her and pet her
love her and pet her and love her and love her
be her friend and pet her
        and play with her and love her
and watch her fucking die and forget all about her until you see the picture
"a part of us"
codie you were my favorite

why is Elena in 50% of my dreams?
why will i never forget her?
moving on

random and thoughtless, useless and dreadful

those small patches of light
        thousands of feet below you flying high
all of those people and houses
        you'll never see or meet
san diego twice in a year
find the bracelet on the floor of the barracks
not knowing i'll wear it
        nonstop for four years and counting
not knowing the 311 room thing will come to a head
almost dying in the salty sea on a california beach
touching a girl you were crushing on
after a day of competition
        and loving every minute of it
the trees around you freeze and fall
        and your past dies in a day
not remembering what places looked like
        whenever you loved them
not caring about them now when you don't notice them or love them
but just see
        what they are no longer
i    i    i    i have
        (insert Pink Floyd lyric)
biddy diddy bop (a bop diddy biddy)
wait, we've already been there
i know this ain't no "Howl"
will? who?
why? when?
i no longer know what it felt like only
        what i think it looked like
fuck those posh flannel wearing disco bums
junk dealers who teach english to spanish kids
i don't know what i know
        and wish i didn't know what i don't
gilmour is playing the ultimate
making my eyes cum with tears
the pic noise from string plucking
Will looking so at home inside a car's engine compartment
Kirk's glow of guitar playing
Tim's ecstatic charisma when talking of Colin or Digby
together they make me sane and warm
i love these men and their laughs and smiles
        make tomorrow worth waiting for
        and my past worth dealing with

unlike feminist porn stars who take it in their ears
at oak park one time with Brianna and Kirk i saw some kids kissing
and i yelled "stick it in her ear!"
i still laugh
much like when Kirk and i see and say pak halal
although he calls me a "fucking eskimo"
    and rams the heater
    all the way up in my truck
talking shit about the parking spots i choose
"geez we need a shuttle to take us
    from our car to the store."
but it's cool because he was there when it started
they all were and will be
the day my fortress wasteland began its construction
no judgment, only concern
only care, no questioning
        aaaaaaaaaaaaaaaahhhhhhhhhh!
licking nipples is interesting and tasty
i'm a crazy fucking prick
one thought and silly anecdote at halsey
one funny idea and quirky anecdote at 51$^{st}$
and now two years of stress and brainstorming
it did need to be so high i see that now
and it'll only get bigger and stronger
jack jacky jack my buddha bud
where's desolation?
hey jim, shoot it in my toe
henry, spot me 'til my pecs burst out
    emotion and words
for a few months i'd take prozac and zoloft
    and go into a daze
with zoloft you yawn without an orgasm to end it
    and your teeth chatter
    and jaw aches and sometimes you dry heave
it is as fun as it sounds
prozac is great and i wish i had a reason to take it
all i need to calm me is a good scream and cry
    to force out my demon
    and sob myself to sleep

healthy healthy bitty iddy biznatch
fuck why do we learn to systemize each other
categorize and rank

eh, i got nothing else to do
        but fall constantly from grace
        and lie to a god that hates me
you can reach me now
i won't reach back & i won't run
if you want me dead come live in my mind
        and see it's not far off

## 9-11

if i had a machine
    that let me travel back through time
i'd collect all of the tears fallen from then until today
    then hover over the parallel edifices
        so tall they scrape the heavens
i'd pour the uncountable tears
    on top of our burning past
and hopefully one more life would walk out
    with a new batch of tears in their eyes


## pessi

people base their views of others
    on what they've done and not who they are
i'm sure hundreds of people dislike me
    because of how they know of me
yet no one truly knows me
i know i do it too
i look back on people in high school and how i never liked them
    based on a thing they said or did
will we ever learn to not judge
    but just enjoy each other?

## curfew

for bark bark

darling i know you can't stay
but please before you go
tell me that you love me
i need to hear it so
hug me so tight tonight
so hard i'll almost fall
in your arms i feel so warm
and i know all will be okay
just go, although
i never wanna let go
just go
we'll be together tomorrow
touch your lips to mine
make it last for all time
just go
you can't be late anymore
just go, although
i'll miss your touch
just go, although
i'll be alone
just go
i'll see you in my dreams

## larisa oleynick blues

the most amazing eyes i've ever seen
you're my sexy-baby movie queen
you've stunned my heart since '94
sad not to see you anymore

back then i knew i loved you
back then i knew i cared
i remember my heart hurting and constricting
knowing you'll never be there

a thousand nights alone in bed
a vision of you and i
on a white sand beach
in a far-off land

cuddling in a field of grass
a hundred-year-old tree to mark
the spot where we'll first kiss
the spot to recall what i'll always miss

you are in my soul and in my heart
i would give a million stars for one day with you
i would give my lifetime of love
to see one night through
       in you
the secret world i created
in the deepest part of my mind
you sit on a golden throne, jewel encrested
my sexy-baby movie queen
someday can i be your king?

## a farewell to tripsy

she doesn't see me for good looks
    and i sure don't have the wealth
it took time but those misconceptions of me
    were stacked upon her shelf

i fear those hot nights years ago
    will fade into the dark
all i need now is not to think about
    your breathing and your moaning
    in those spots that we would park

don't go away my lovely
    the darkness will too soon come
i can't stand to see your back turn darling
    don't say the words "we're done."
    don't say the words "we're done."
    don't say the words "we're done."

'cause i know in time your heart will heal
    and then your eyes will dry
and i will grow to be your shining star
    coming from far across the sky
to carry you into the forever ever after
    don't say the words "we're done."
    don't say the words "we're done."
i wonder in bed with the lights down low
    what you tell your friends about me
    what all do they know?
i can't see your smile in my mind now
    just the tears and pain i caused
i wonder what tomorrow will bring
    perhaps an end to our love that never was

she didn't see the good looks
    and i sure didn't give her time
years have passed and the lost misconceptions
    are off the shelf and back in her mind
    don't say the words "we're done."
    don't say the words "we're done."

i miss you and i'm sorry
sorry that our day will never come

### the tetherball ding

i dream i was you
and you'd give all to be in my shoes
your eyes are so wide and amazing
mine are so dark and dead

the playground of your life will soon be a wasteland of regret
play all you can today
for tomorrow you will be twenty and me
and then there's no turning back

don't try and grow up too fast
you'll miss everything that will become what
        you think about when you don't want to die
days will fly by my child
live for every second
        live for every fucking thing
live for you and now
don't think about me
i'll be fine
somehow

## sixty six

in dreams the angel dies
with a mouthful of dragonflies
inside it blows my mind
until the end of time

the virgin sees the tree
and rides the devil's bee
i stay upon the tracks
and sniff the scent of frost
the breeze cracks and rabbits smile
jesus stays a while

soon the light will end
soon will come again
see the darkened lizard
upon the flowing hills
across the boiling ponds
it all ends with a bang
it all ends and we dance naked
and it all ends and we kiss
the virgin, the angel, and us
it all ends with the loss of today

### june 6th, 2002 - thursday

i don't know where to go when i'm all alone and dreaming of you

---

i want to be an animal
and rip the veins from your face
with a dying elm branch
tied to the end of my mace

---

i figured we could try and sound like other bands and fail. or try our own sound and ride it 'til we reach the edge of the world. and possibly turn around to see the people of the world behind us, or continue over the edge into insanity

---

flickering lights on the wall of your home on the very first night we ever touched

---

i—i don't remember if it was friedrich nietzsche or—or—or mr. seever on an old episode of 'growing pains' who—who said and i'm—i'm quoting here, "boner, put down that cat." well, i guess that's my outlook on life.

## bourgeoisie

**xxi**

nothing is hard if you try
most of us give in and die
everything changes they say
luckily tomorrow is a new day

**xxii**

whipple whipple whipping winds
running running runny rains
muddy adobe flapping breeze
sunflowers glisten     sunny days
sunlight raze and a magenta haze
all time is glorious
all love is pure
kiss me and wish for eternity

**xxiii**

filing down the anthill
sandy silt and dirt
back to my life's contention
back to my day's work

**xxiv**

too many loves are dangerous
too much sex absurd
take your time with loving
and always keep your word

**xxv**

and he said "i love you"
and kissed his daughter's head
she smiled and the tears rained
tomorrow they'll do the same

**xxvi**

through my veins runs blackness
and hatred tenfold
i'll never stop 'til i can't breath
and my body is bloated and cold

### traffic

the dark will creep
and blood will seep
into your unclean eye
see all of your deceit
gaze upon your betrayal
fuck your demon
rape your heart
the dark will seep
the blood will creep
there is no running
from what you have done
your end will be coming
fear it

## bourgeoisie

**xxvii**
it's a fucked-up world we live in
where the dumb control us all
and the brilliant minds and poets
are tallying prison walls

**xxviii**
power can not be created
but deferred from time to time
often it takes a few words
something simple like a rhyme

**xxix**
there is a demon in my conscience
and i smell its stench of fear
it stabs me and i kill it
a part of me always dies

**xxx**
surrounded by mistakes
encircled by the future
i know i'll hurt much more
both myself and many others
do i deserve to live if i cause pain?
do i deserve to die if i'm insane?
do i cry because i feel bad?
or is it because i want to?
someday it'll all end
with a bang through the top
of my fucked-up skull

**xxxi**
death is a dream
fear is your past
hate is your savior
love is your tormentor
friends are your downfall

**xxxii**
tomorrow in dreams i die
tomorrow the children cry
yesterday was delight
in a year i'll end the fight

_____**shook the pillars of heaven** *
you're using me.
        i'm helping you.
you're hurting me.
        you hurt me.
that was then, this is now.
        so you can hurt people and i can't?
you have a choice, i made one. this is the present and you can stop if you want.
        why should i?
so you won't regret it in a year from now like i do for what i did.
        it's hard not to hurt you
        because i'm struggling not to love you.
but you do love me.
        i know, and it's killing me.
i love you.
        i love you, too.
good night sweet girl.
        farewell, my lovely.


_____**july 15th, 2002 - monday**
this moment forever yesterday
tomorrow always forgotten

## the last kiss

for my "best friend" Will's girlfriend

it began in the hallway, a number,
    some paper, a pen
it all started in this moment when
we caught each other's glance
in this moment we saw a chance
and that chance we took
without a second look
the first night on The Futon
love blossomed watching 'Leon'
inside us a bond was forming
to take us to a place unforeseen
in each other we found that one thing
the missing thing we need
you poked me and flirted and i said
"you know where that'll lead"

i saw you while i was sleeping
i saw you when i dreamed
you kissed me and i loved you
not knowing what you saw in me
i gave my class ring to you to give back on the day
when our love would take a new step
"freak on a leash" leading the way

too soon after i hurt you
too soon i fell from grace
to this day i remember
your broken angel face
to this day i can recall
your eyes burning through me
as i leaned against the wall

we shared a long time together
through hot seasons, long years, cold weather
we spent a long time as one
i never thought we'd be done
i look back at who i was then
and also at who you were
you were always the better of us
i never did add up to much

snow will fall in old town
our memories i'll tear down
your sweet smile i still remember
do you think of me at all?
i wish someday you'd call
there was a light inside you
and with me you always shared
i hurt you and i hurt you, i don't know why
but still i truly cared

in the sunlight on the water that one day
        at the lake
i saw a sparkle in your squinting eyes
and a smile you couldn't fake
i wish i was more for you
i wish i'd shown more love
in the end a better man you made me
like an angel from above

the silver watch still ticks
ticks away the time i spend alone
the words engraved are too close for comfort
i cry sometimes at home
"i seek fantasies, seek dreams" which ends with
"visions surround, but no truth"
come to me and love me that infamous
        one fine day
only your kiss can soothe

the picture frame with all our pet names
stares me through the night
the glowing frogs hang from the ceiling
they let me know it will be all right
as i scribe this now you're not mine
you are in his arms

someday i'll be able to live with that

he'll never treat you like i did
all my embarrassing stories i hid
maybe he'll give you truth
maybe he'll give you love

in his arms you may fit tightly
like a warm mitten or a glove

outside his house your car sits
(do you remember when i first took you there?)
at my house alone i wait
re-falling in love with my best friend's girlfriend
the guilt is a pressing weight
i will fight it if you help me
i need you oh so bad
i loved you and i still do
now though you're the love i cannot have

too soon i did hurt you
too soon from grace i fell
i look forward to what the future holds
our fate will someday tell
in my dreams i see you
you smile in the kansas sun
in my dreams i kiss you
for our time apart is done

## hard-core / on-core

(stage is empty, lights low, brett walks on and sits in the center)

father: i don't know what happened to my boy. he used to be smart and energetic. now he's just a lazy piece of shit and a joke. he never did put forth effort or stick with anything. he's a loser.

mother: he used to be my darling little boy. my little boy was so nice and sweet to everyone. now he doesn't speak or treat anyone with respect. i don't know what happened.

friend: he liked to think that everyone owed him for everything. that he was the leader and that he took care of us and was so fucking superior. he thought we were stupid and didn't think we could do things on our own. i didn't think friends should be like that. i've not seen him in a while and i really don't care.

brother: he used to amaze me with all of the stuff he knew about movies, books and music even. i was so proud for a while that i was his brother. i was always telling my friends about him and about his talents as a writer and such. i don't think he ever cared about me. i think he feels that i was a disgrace to him because of all of the stupid things i did. it may be true but i never stopped loving him for who he was. i love him even if he despises me.

friend 2: brett was always the passionate one, wanting everyone, all of us guy friends, to be together and to never separate. he did act like he cared and felt for us. it's just too bad it really was an act. that mother-fucker was the first one to bail on our group and now no one talks anymore and i do blame it all on him. the selfish mother-fucker. fuck him!

classmate: brett? yeah, i remember him, he, well, i always thought he was gay and so did a lot of other people. i don't know why, he just always seemed to be a fuckin' pussy, ya know? doing fuckin' ROTC and that kind of shit. i didn't know him personally really, i just knew of him and of his reputation, that asshole fucked over a lot of people. nobody really liked him.

father: he thought he was smarter than us and that i was a dumbshit for not ever doing more with my life. who is he to talk, i couldn't even get him to fuckin' mow the lawn or do the dishes, he just would sit upstairs in his room watching dvd's that he would spend all of his money on. he was like a damned vampire, rarely leaving except to go to work, and even there he didn't do much but sit around and start movies.

classmate 2: i remember he knew everything about movies, if you ever need an answer to a movie question just ask him, it really was all he was good for. i don't know why or how he knew all of that stuff, he probably didn't have a real life and would sit around watching movies all day and looking them up on the internet.

teacher: i think he had tremendous talent in writing and with movie stuff, but he wasn't much of a go-getter. he would always talk about these grandiose things he wanted to do but would never come through on them. yeah, he was a rather big disappointment.

mother: i would always get on the computer and see the internet sites he would go to and it was a lot of totally disgusting porno stuff. he has a sick fascination with it and that always upset me. i think he is addicted to sex and that is not tolerable.

ex-girlfriend: we dated a long time ago, like in middle school and the first year or so of high school. he would always tell me he loved me, but would never take me anywhere or buy me dinner and a movie. in fact he never even really kissed me in public or at school. it was like he was embarrassed to show affection. a lot of my friends thought he was fag, but i don't know. whenever we'd talk on the phone all he'd want to talk about was sex and me giving him a blow job. none of which ever happened. i didn't care, i would have done the stuff but he never gave me time or actually saw me.

friend 3: he was there when i really needed him, i went through a bad spell and having him around always made me feel better. i did notice a change in him but i didn't feel like it was my place to do anything about him. basically he was just fuckin' himself over with his relationship and all of that. he deserved the pain he got for breaking that girl's heart.

ex-girlfriend 2: we dated for a little over two years and it was good at times, but i never felt that he loved me. we wanted different things and he wasn't as faithful as one should be. one day he would tell me he loved me, and then go out and sleep with some whore. we'd break up and he'd cry and i'd feel bad and take him back. yeah, this happened about four times and, fuck him, i didn't deserve that. i could still be his friend because he was there when i needed him for the most part, but i think he just liked my body and never really considered anything serious.

ex-girlfriend 3:          i wasn't really his girlfriend. i met him once and we went out a little bit after that and he was my first kiss and basically my first everything. i let him kiss me and then he touched me and he wanted to keep goin' and so by this point i didn't care. he basically used me to get off and it hurt me a lot. every time we got together it seemed that i would be on my period, so he'd spend all night jackin' off and using my body as a target. it was fine i guess, but thinking back on it now it was rather pathetic on his part.

ex-girlfriend 2:          i do think that he started to love me for real as we dated longer and longer, but he fucked me over one too many times and only after he lost me did he fully realize that i was what he wanted. guess what? it's way too late, so fuck off!

friend:          i always knew that brett had a thing for girls and sometimes that really irritated me. he would leave hanging out at my house to go be with some bimbo and then come back and expect us to be fine with it. and then he cheated on his girlfriend who was friends with us and he thought we wouldn't say anything. well, we turned out to care more for her than he did. which is why i'm dating her now and it's perfect.

classmate:          i didn't know him well i just knew that not many people liked him. they thought he was always trying to act like he was a lot bigger and more popular than he was. as far as loser goes, he was right there.

father:          when he was young he played soccer but didn't stick with it, then he played baseball and quit, took piano for a year and quit and then karate for about three years, but we paid for five so he cost me a few grand there. he never could come through with anything. like his writings he does in the basement. he's done it for about five or so years now and i've never read anything. you'd think he'd show me something by now. i don't know, he isn't who he used to be and i wish he would stop making our lives miserable.

friend:          i wish he'd stop wallowing in his own self-pity and wake up to the fact that no one feels sorry for him and that we don't care anymore. he left us and ran out and we have stopped loving him. surprisingly it wasn't that different.

girlfriend 2:    i'm glad that we broke up because it made me see that if i try and make the wrong guy fit into my dream, then i end up only hurting myself. brett is different and he thinks he is special and acts like he is the only person who has felt pain. i don't care anymore, he can be depressed and hurt all he wants, it makes me feel better.

mother:    he used to be the blond boy all of the little girls wanted to kiss. now, and i hate to admit this, he is a liar and a cheater and i wish someone would break his heart again just to make him pay. my little boy is a prick and he will soon get his.

father:    i thought my first son messed up, well i was surprised to see brett turn out this way. as far as it goes now, i only have one son, because he actually cares about others and about living a good life. brett is too busy worrying about himself, hate, fear and death. when he dies i'm sure he'll do it himself and i still won't go to his funeral. he had a cute little girlfriend and we'd always say, "what does she see in you?" or "how the hell did you get a girl like her?" she was an angel and he screwed her over and ran her away. it seems to me that he likes to run off all of the people that care about him. oh, well, good-bye son.

(brett screams on stage)

brett:    aaaaaaaaaaaaaaahhhhhhhhhhhhhhhhhh!!!!!!!!

(a gunshot is heard)

## jo-co son-flower

little baby on mother's shoulders
growing older it's getting colder
i fear you sometimes
i'm afraid that you'll hate me
promise me we'll stay together

little baby in arms rocking
sixty-eight years, death comes knocking
momma love me i need it so
show me the light in your eye
in the end i love you, don't cry

i don't know where i went wrong
why i fucked up so bad
i don't know why i do these things i do
i can't understand why i hate you
the sun does burn
the moon will fall
a look you once gave me, a word said
will destroy it all

momma tell me that you love me
momma is there someone up above?
i want to feel the presence and be sure
touch the light and not be a failure
why do i feel this hate?
why do i want to die?
why do i long to hurt?
why do i love my pain?
i need to say i love you
before it takes me away

little baby in cradle rocking
little baby in casket dreaming
soon the sun will burn through
everything we share
did you ever care?
the sun does burn
the moon will fall
a look you once gave me, a word said
has destroyed it all

momma tell me that you love me
momma is there someone up above?
i want to feel the presence and be sure
touch the light and not be a failure
in your eyes
in your eyes
in your eyes
little baby (in your eyes)
little child (touch the light)
little baby (in your eyes)
little child (touch the light)

walk with me into the sun
walk with me into the sun
walk with me into the sun
walk with me into the sun

my child i love you
it is done

## 31 stoplights
for Ainsley •

ten miles
twenty minutes
but a thousand worlds away
in your bedroom
thinking and dreaming of me
a universe i've never known
you showed me the city
you made me feel like a suburban fool
i think of you
and i scare myself
i don't know what will be
a universe away
a past i'll never know
encounters i'll never see
twenty minutes
ten miles
you're not too far from me

## giNgEr bridge

atop my rusty epitaph
i can see for miles and miles
the rollercoaster where we first met
the isle of capris where we gambled
        on your 21st birthday
the cityscape and towers behind me
        where i made my fortune

the wind is chilly today
i can feel the metal swaying
the river park where we walked
        and planned our future
our first kiss underneath
        the parking lot light at 12:34

this structure is like us
it has history
it can tell stories from the past
it has been broken and mended, like we have
next week they plan to tear it down
        and build a new one

like you

i can see the lofts where he lives and where i saw you
on the front steps kissing and in his arms
what about our farm house?
what about our horse?
what about the children we'd adopt?
what is sadder, me now at this moment
or the fact that everybody driving by sees me
but doesn't stop to help?
enough wondering, it's a minute 'til that time
the time i fall into the flowing cold
which we will never share
good-bye
12:34

## _____**comedy?**_____
### for a facsimile of an ex-lover

i long for your caring
i feel the need for you
you once kissed my cheek
in the ocean on the beach
your skin was sandy
but hands were smooth
god i miss you

your dog cody once licked me
during a picnic in the park
from the tower we saw our future
from the future we saw our love
we fell asleep in the lot
after your late night at work
we didn't touch but just lied thinking
thinking we'd never part

dark night at your parent's house
through your window i climbed
this was the first time we became invincible
the last time though, we cried
i can smell your scent on my bed sheets
i can see you when i sleep
except i've not slept in weeks

you write me poems and i love them
send me pictures that i adore
i long for your caring
i feel the need for more
does it hurt to remember
what it felt like in our bed?
is it awkward to recall
what i looked like naked?
or do you try to forget it all?
god i swear i miss you

at a restaurant through a window i saw you
laughing, smiling, and looking in his eyes
does he buy you things i never did?
does he send you random gifts or flowers?

take you places you always wanted to go?
say things that i never said?
i'm sure he does
but does he love you like i do?
i'm sure he does
why did you leave me?
god i swear i miss you
but for now
our tomorrow in my mind
is gold

## 79th street cistern

forever we cry
the lover's tears of never
never we touch
the terror of friends at end
wrap me 'round your finger
comfort my everything
it stings to see my own face
snarling in the black water
rushing through kansas veins
channeled through all forgiveness
represent my fate
reciprocate my hate
die beneath the streets
swim in the sand
i'll never be your man
tell me nothing all day tomorrow
cut the lawn of my un-mowed past
terrorize self-control
demonize self-penetration
forever we cry
never we touch
comfort my everything
hello my dear, good-bye
the waste is running too high

## the snow fell in kansas

the streetlights are on
the traffic lights are blinking
it's midnight
and you're not here

in my home town
traffic lights would run all night
just like you do now
parks would close from 12:00 to 5:00
but we'd hide in the bushes
from the light
you were there and we made love
it was dark and our hearts we bright

the weather vane is spinning
the rain gauge overflows
it's dawn and i ask
"where is she?"
i'm scared, because no one knows

tree leaves would fall
in my childhood's yard
we'd rake and jump on them all
the cherry tree planted in 1st grade
was struck on a stormy night in july
it crashed to the ground
taking with it my youth
all i can ask is "why?"

kids we were when we met
that day at the jungle gym
that day the Challenger fell to the ocean
that day i fell for you

the train tracks are shaking
the whistle blows hard
your kisses on my eyelids are forever
and so is us lying in my yard

the breeze is subtle in old town
the lights illuminate your smile
we put a penny on the tracks

pressed in denver in '68
we stood back from the track to wait
it took forever
but at least we were together

your bare back in the moonlight was amazing
the nights alone in my bed
the greatest thing i regret
is forgetting what you had said
something about "forever ... "
something about "our love ... "
something about "infinity's power ... "
something about "our love ... "

the breeze is subtle in old town
the whistle blows hard
tree leaves will fall
the traffic lights will blink
i'll give way for you

will you ever give me the time?

## lady in white*

breathe
       if you think that it's me
speak
       if you don't want to see
touch
       i know where you'll be
listen
       there's not much more of you and me

we gave it up
we passed away
cashed in our tokens
and blew our wad on hope
many things we went through
many problems solved
we were to always be together
when did it all go away?

on tuesdays i stay home from work
and drink until i can't think straight
on wednesdays i sleep in all day
i'm getting too impatient to wait
you told me you dream of a day in the future
in the rain we could meet again
it's true
but what you didn't think about
is what to do 'til then

no one will ever be you
in my eyes you were perfect
no one can replace you
now i can barely face you

i fucked a girl a week ago
and my body felt so cold
i'm doing things that will keep you from me
your mistakes i've never told

after we went our own way
promising to return
we did things with no concern
things to keep us both from wanting

to come back together
i've done more than you

nothing will ever be the same again
it can never be like it was
you left me and then found my best friend
your hooking up has begun his and my end
and i fucking despise you for it
as much as i want you back

### t.v. screen glow on naked teenage bodies

4:08 in the morning
i doubt i'll go to sleep
i'm surrounded by darkness
outside the window lightning strikes
Dreamer's "everything" plays and i'm depressed
we will never have anything like what Randy sings about

reading through your letters tonight
we had so much love
still i saw how horrible i was to you
all of the clues and also solutions
were right there in your words
i never listened
you told me about communication
about listening and being there more
about reciprocity in a relationship
i can do that now
i learned from the pain of losing you
and if i ever get to test what i learned
it's a waste that it won't be on you

4:13 my lamp is on
the bulb in it has burned for almost two years
we burned for two years
and i'm the only one still burning
eventually we ended and the light ceased
soon the bulb will die
like our love

4:14
i love you and we're over still

## a floor that glows in blacklight
on my floor i often find
long red hairs from one amazing night
two kids surrounded by pleasure

my futon has small stains from the juices of another girl
we did everything you could imagine to one another
and she left with my juice all over her breasts

several, almost dozens of conquests
have been encountered in this very room
girls i've perhaps only met once
and usually haven't seen since
used each other for an orgasm or two

licking the sweat from a young girl's body
can be better than the sex itself
just the knowledge of knowing that i made them sweat
and made them cream    is good
i adore their scent on my fingers
the smell of the air afterwards
"it smells like ... victory."

in hindsight it is only defeat

the quick jerking of their arms
the vibrating of their legs
the pumping of their crotch
the quivering of their whole body
the bristling of their hair entangled in mine
the smooth caressing of the small of their backs

pain and pleasure tear up in me often
when their nails dig in my side
or right above my elbow
it feels good anywhere
but what's best is when their tongue is used instead
the moments when the clothes come off is so extraordinary
that nothing hardly comes close
except the smug smiles on our faces
as we put them back on

## side board

enclosure seems so inviting
isolation i want to feel
all i have in my life drains me
everything needs to die

tell me something my angel
anything good that i have done
the world is strangling me
the light burns me through

take me into the dark forest
and shroud me from the sun
cover me in darkness
so i can begin my descent
into my mind

let the memories destroy me
allow my dreams to die
and turn cold
skin away my drive to ever be anything
toss my hunk of flesh into the water

just let me float
and be nothing
let me die inside
let me be saved from the pain

frame my flesh in glass
and let my friends come see what i am now
what i have become
my eyes will still work
and i will still comprehend
i can and shall see their faces
my muscles won't work
so they can't see me smile
i will laugh at their pain

the tears will fall to the ground
and my heart will still be dead

## the guy across the room
for Shauna

such a long time has passed
i don't see you
and haven't in a year and a half
i first saw you three years back
"cute as a button" they say and so do i
you were so young and sweet, beautiful
i wanted to know you and show you life
but i was with someone and you were so young
you called me once and only once
we talked for a little while
at the same time my girlfriend
        was giving me head
i was turned on by talking to you
        while she was gobbling me
looking at it all now i wonder
how much have you changed?
what has life done to you?
have you been corrupted by this world?
i recall being disappointed
        by you not having a writing piece
        in our class' collection
"i don't have anything to remember you by" i said.
you scribbled down "remember me, Shauna"
        on a note
which is still in my wallet
i dreamt about you and your sister a few times
and that's all i'm gonna say
perhaps it's good that i don't know you now
maybe you are different
maybe you have been fucked over
        and are living in your shell
since i don't know you now i can live
        with the vision of who you were
what i make you out to be in my head
you are beautiful, Shauna
i still want to read the poem you wrote about me

## is frenchy home?

Elliott Smith is singing and i am mystified
my mind is being fucked by alcohol and i am deified
"what a fucking joke!"
thank you Elliott, good comment
i feel like i have nothing
i am not who i was
nor am i who i want to be
and i am not who i act like i am
i read some Selby and some Rollins tonight
i have their darkness inside me
i just can't articulate it as well
if i try to delve into my pain or drink my soul away
it will merely be because
        i want to have the façade of doing that
not because i am really doing that
i dwell on the one who said he was my friend
and then carved into my back
        the truth of how he wasn't
i dwell on the girl who i held for two years
and now spends her nights with my ex-best friend
they are happy and in love, loving and touching
all at the cost of my soul and sanity
do they know these things hurt me? yes
do they try to help me? no.
do they want to? no.
"they don't know what to do." i am told
they are too busy ignoring us for their world
to try and help me from destroying myself
just let me kill my mind
let me fuck away all anguish through the body
of someone who loves me but i don't love
i want to hurt people who are good to me
        because people have hurt me
i want to fuck sweet little girls to fuck them over
        and destroy their sweetness
to end the rage of my head

fourteen years of fucking friendship
traded on a chance for the woman whom i love
fourteen years of friendship thrown away
we used to ride bikes, destroy property
now we ride the edge of a brawl

and destroy our childhood
we used to go camping and dream about our future
we were gonna build houses next to each other
and have our kids be friends throughout their childhood
we were gonna ...
we were gonna ...
Will?    Will?
can you hear me?
please Will i fucking loved you and you hurt me
tell me why?  why?
what did i do?
did i do something to you
        to make you stab me in the back
        and destroy our past?
remember our little claymation movie we made?
wise monkey productions?
do you remember going to hibachi?
i fucking loved you
        and you killed everything good i ever had
you were the light of my life
i looked up to you because you were a great man
        and a great influence
i tried hard to save you from drinking yourself to death
and in return you hurt me and now i have succumbed
        to the charms of the bottle
Will?    Will?    can you hear me?
i am alone and standing on the black bloody wasteland
        of our childhood
Will?    it's dark and i can't see
i feel everything fading away
Will?    there isn't much time
give me a hand or some light
help me please, Will?
i'll die in a moment or so if you don't help
Will?    hey Will?         speak no evil?
we are always going to be together right?
it's always going to be tuesday at my house, right?
Will?    the darkness is outside my door now
come on don't joke with me
Will?    help me?
Will ...    Will ...

i'm done crying over you

## 311/317

forgive my thankfulness
my frankness and brutality
forget my loveliness
my sweetness and humility
everything i gave you is gone
and i am here a drunken fool
swimming in a pool of my own shallow remorse
tell me how you want me to die
for i will do it
tell me if you want me to live on
for i shall do it
the only thing i will not do
is stand by and watch you love him


## apocryphal

tundra love with albino features
silly creatures under the sun
myriad dialects guide the fall
towers of romanticism the templars guard
from the yard the bulldog yells
ringing bells from the chambers of evermore
an angel bellows to his mighty friend
a long-lost theologian man

tell me strong, tell me true
what is, what shall, and what will we do?
dogma and rituals
rites and masonic rule
realize your knowledge and do not waste it
a fool is one who can not use his tools

deep in the sand of egypt
a haunting vision, a sight
a young pharaoh rulers remains
are a key item in a 10,000-year-old fight
throw out past discrepancies
forget all old codes
the one above only loves
so love him

## i got first swing!
### based on a true story

the boy was the first one
his friend was the last one
no one was in-between
they awoke before the rooster screamed
and met at their school's playground
one brought the shells
the other brought the instrument of their end

on the swings they sat for mere minutes
going over their reason, their cause
covering all questions
remembering their childhood
      on this very swing set
a little sun began to shine
but before the light was warm
the first boy took the gun barrels into his mouth
and off his face went
his best friend urinated in his pants
      and began to freak out and cry
but before he had time to reconsider
in the gun went and out his brain came

the first boy survived and his face was rebuilt
he now looks like a puppet
he was on t.v. talking about his reasons
yeah, it did sound like bullshit

**ill-loom-a-naughty fetish**

where do i go from here?
what do i do now?
who do i have?
when will it go away?
how can i make it through the night?

she is gone from my life
i will never be over her
she haunts me and i scream
i think i no longer dream
not only of her
anyone or anything
i ran out of dreams

i don't even have nightmares
sometimes they were better anyway
it often can be better to see visions of things you fear
than to see things you want and will never have

where do i go from here?
    hell
what do i do now?
    wait for pain and death
who do i have?
    only yourself
when will it go away?
    when death comes calling
how can i make it through the night?
    you won't

he is outside your door

## god bless american't

i am a man who failed
who had a relationship that failed
i am a child of a marriage that failed
in a failing family
in a failing country
on a failed planet

they say, "brett, you can't live life without hope!"
oh ho ho, i have hope
i hope every time she kisses him
        she can feel the two years she gave up
and the fourteen years of friendship he threw away
i hope that when she sees him
        she envisions what it used to look like
when he and i would walk together
and now sees me dark
        and brooding ready to strike from behind
i hope that when he holds her she remembers
the arms that used to be around her
arms that are now connected to trembling hands
        writing down words
        that are seeds of hate
arms that made her warm
        and are now attached to a frozen shell
        of a once-warm man
i hope my parents never find happiness
i hope our country commits reverse suicide
and has its brains blown back into our heads

## _____ won't grow on chalk *

i see you there
you look at me
i wonder
do you like what you see?
you're sitting close
here next to me
your hair smells sweet
will this be what i want it to be?
a weekend passes
then a month or two
it once was you and then me
but now it's me with you

you stand here you're so pretty
you hold my hands and it sets me free
touch me, kiss me
love me into eternity

you walk away
you leave me here
you love him now
not me anymore
it kills my soul and i curse your name
i'll never be the same
i wish you'd hate me
cause now i hate you
and i don't want you anymore
but i do, and it hurts
so fuck you
you left me here all alone
and you love him, as i turn to stone
why won't you love me?
why can't you save me?
why did you do this to ... us?

## i sat in a penguin with a goat: a love story
### for 4-helly

we met in a time where i was very confused
you fell for me very quick
    and harder than you will ever admit
i only saw you, in the beginning at least
as something to play with and forget about later
we did many things that we shouldn't have
because of your age and my girlfriend at the time
    but we did them anyway
remember the pool parking lot
    with the rain pouring down?
    yeah "white socks", i get it, ha ha
what about the early morning around 2 a.m.
    it was chilly
i came and got you, the church parking lot?
sometimes i would see you and hate myself
and i know often you would see me and hate yourself
for not allowing yourself to get what you want
    but give me what i wanted
i enjoyed going to 'the nutcracker' with you
and i'm sorry i threw that sandwich out the window
    i have anger inside me sometimes
i wish you would let me open doors for you more
    and i wish you would unlock the door
    of my truck from the inside
you gave me a letter once that i read at taco bell
right before i went to see Ben Folds
months later we sat at the same taco bell
    in the same seat
and i told you about reading your letter there
in your letter you said
    that listening to "Change" by Good Charlotte
    would reveal some of your thoughts
    and feelings
i wrote back and quoted lyrics from
    "Straw Dog" by Something Corporate
i said that you often represented the darkness
    darkness that drove me
    to do detrimental things
that back when we messed around
    what we did would drive me from the light

who knew come one year later
    that everything cherished by me then
    would be the things that hurt me now
and that you would now be the only light in my life
the time at Eric's house we lied on the couch
    looking into each other's eyes
i asked you "why do you put up with me?"
and you stroked my head and told me
    "because of moments like this."
when it comes to the mentality of society
what we have is looked down upon
    because of your age
it is sad to think that the ones
    who don't like the idea of you and me
    are the ones that destroy you as a person
i often feel like i am the only one
    who sees the good in you
on the phone one time
    we both listened to a song called "Everything"
mine was by Dreamer
yours was by Lifehouse
both of us can relate the song to the other
the road we have traveled this past year has been very bumpy
    on both sides
we can both be in moods
    where we are hurtful to the other
yet we still smile whenever our eyes connect
i joke with you about you being in love with me
i try to get you to say it but you won't
you don't need to
i know you do
and i feel the same way

in our future i can predict us saving each other

### **red rover red rover your childhood is over**
foursquare fellatio
swing-set swingers
kickball coitus
played the games of your wonder years
playing the games now that get you nowhere
your first kiss to your first fuck
it used to be about the cute girl
now it's about the easy one
it once was stay out 'til 10:30 p.m.
      and cover the town in fun
now it's "where the hell were you last night?"
      and cover your ass and cock
one minute she is in a dance class performance
then in a dorm room, it's dark
and she can't remember his name
you were so nervous your first time
these days the only excitement
      is being with a new partner
exploring the creeks in the snow is over
adventuring through threesomes
      and orgies is key now
why? is this all there is in life after childhood?
you go to the mall and you can see sex everywhere
you can fucking smell it
it is being sold right next to 'newsweek'
i want to go back to then
back to before
to care about the person first
not their willingness
i don't want to just fuck them
i want to know them and not feel any desire
but allow the desire to build
      and then comes the physical

i'm so fucking off track right now
i am repeating myself
i am losing my way
just forget it all
everything you have is fleeting
fuck everyone you can and exploit it
run yourself into the ground or over the edge
and take some assholes like me with you

from tether ball to cunnilingus
from finger-paints to fingering cunts
old things die
new things are born
both will fucking end you
leave me be i'm going insane

## shoelaces, david taylor, and a new found glory shirt

tonight in your car i was singing along
    with "Overdue" by The Get Up Kids
and you couldn't help but look at me and smile
    as i squeezed your thigh
your sister was in the back seat and commented on
    how bright your face would light up
and how big your beautiful eyes would grow
    when i touch you
"i have that power" i said
who would've known that tonight
    would be the first time
    that you would say "i love you" to me
you simply mouthed the words but it still counts
i never would have expected though
    that the first time you said those words
you would be sitting in a ditch on the roadside
    with your head split open
with me standing before you
    covered in yours and my blood
those big beautiful eyes of yours
    swollen shut and bleeding

earlier we sat on the concrete of the skate park
i held you and kept you warm
i said that "there has never been anyone
    that i wanted to hold so close for so long"
i asked what we were going to do about us
you still are way too young
the night started off so powerful
    and then some small sprinkles fell
as i held you close and tried to kiss your cheek
    you pulled away
both emotionally and physically
    and you shelled yourself up
"don't do this" i said
you told me that i shouldn't worry
    and that your attitude
    had nothing to do with me
it's not that i thought you were lying
    i just didn't believe you
"don't do this" i said
you retreated into yourself

i could tell because i do the same thing
i said that "you need to get rid
    of this constriction in your chest—"
i felt it when you breathed
"you are the only one who can" i added
it began to rain
in many ways it began to rain
a little more than a week ago
    i wrote my first poem about you
after i realized my deep and true feelings for you
it rained that night too
    as we sat in the giant penguin
as we drove away tonight your sister and i knew
    you were pissed off at something
you were very placative and i'm sure us asking
    "what's wrong?" over and over
    didn't help too much
i watched as you fastened your seat belt
    and put the part that goes across your chest
    behind your back like a child does
i didn't put mine on
we turned out of the parking lot
    and you hit the gas
outside it rained
you had something on your mind and were upset
    and instead of talking to us
    you showed us how you felt
there is an old saying that
    "some people can turn your life upside down."
it is normally used figuratively
tonight, it became literal
your sister yelled at you to slow down
    so you hit the gas again
"don't do this" i thought
i saw the curve ahead and automatically
    i judged everything
    the rain
    the slick road, your hostility
    our speed, the curve
not to be superior but i've been driving for awhile
    and i knew we wouldn't make it
even if it wasn't slick i still doubt it
as we rounded the curve our rear-end slipped

and i grabbed the wheel
        to help you counter but it didn't help
we were at least 60 in a 30 on a curve
i saw the rain on the windshield
i heard your sister screaming your name
i saw the ditch and a telephone pole
and then we hit and flipped
you would expect that when this happened
        you would close your eyes
        but i didn't
i saw it all, my legs flipping
        the car spinning
        the window shattering
i felt the glass hitting my face
        and my body smacking the door
i heard everything crumbling and breaking
        and you and your sister screaming
i was silent and i wasn't scared
we finally stopped and we were upside down
my face was numb,
all i could hear now was you screaming
the smell of the smoke from the airbags
my back felt a bit messed up
you were yelling about your arms hurting
        and how you couldn't see
i tried to open a door but a barbed-wire fence blocked it
i tried to smash a window and i failed
all i could hear was you screaming
i wasn't afraid but concerned
        because i thought we were trapped
i heard the rain pouring on the car
        and the car beeping
your sister crawled out of the smashed back window
        and i climbed out
"i can't see, i can't see," was all i heard from you
i yelled your name to make sure you were all right
i grabbed for you to help you out
i saw blood everywhere
i could see your body and the back of your head but
        wasn't sure if you were okay
i reached for you and grabbed you and you winced
        with pain from your arm
i had a bit of fear shoot through me because i couldn't

   see your face
the few seconds of nervous anticipation
    were horribly long
then i saw your angel face
it was smashed and bloody but we got you out
you kept saying your dad is going to kill you
    and that you were sorry
i told you those things didn't matter
you sat down in the ditch and i got a real look at you
although my eyes were open the whole time
    the experience was a blur
you began to cry as i knelt beside you
"you are going to leave me now" is all you said
you were afraid i'd never see you again
i told you all of those things don't matter
    you were okay and we'd be fine
my dress shirt that you held to your head
    was drenched in your blood
and it is now in a ziplock bag in my closet
not that i need a reminder of tonight
    but i want to keep it for some reason
i was never scared
    and i'm still not emotionally disturbed
    but i know it will come
at some points throughout the remainder of the night
    i could stop thinking about it
only for a few seconds though
like a looped-tape it plays and plays in my head
the outcome could have been different
one of us may not have walked away
but the rain stopped right after the wreck
it rained long enough for this to happen
we need to make sure
    we got the message and learn from this
my hands were soaked with blood
    and my body was sore and bruised
yet as i looked through the window of the ambulance
    and saw you lying there
your eyes closed and lips moving
i felt good knowing that i didn't lose you
i can't imagine the affect this will have on you
if i had been driving i know i'd be
    in a totally different emotional state

in my first poem last week for you
    i ended with the line
"in our future i can predict us saving each other"
when i wrote that i never envisioned pulling your bloody body
from an overturned car

tonight was horrible and we will never forget the images,
    the feelings and the smells
above everything i will never forget
    you mouthed "i love you"
it took a car crash but i finally got you to admit it
you are so beautiful, kelly
although earlier you told me to quit saying it
because you refuse to believe
    that there is anything good about you
maybe there isn't
    but you instill good in me
last night i was inside you and covered in your scent
come one day later i am beside you amidst, metal,
    glass, blood, and pain.
at 11:15 tonight we crashed
    as "Walking On A Wire" played
    a fitting song
it's 2:37 a.m. as i finish this
barely three hours later and i forgive you already
we need each other more than ever now
let me in and love me
and let me love you
because i do

now you just need to save me

## understanding thursday on pleasant valley rd.

i barely got any sleep last night
i was beyond tired but when i closed my eyes
all i saw was your bloody body spinning before me
you called at 3:24 a.m. right after you got home
        from the hospital
you asked if i was okay
i am
i began to relax knowing that you were gonna be okay
except for the staples in your head
i came to see you and brought you and your sister
some cards and stuffed frogs
i was more scared walking to your front door
        than i was all last night
your sister led me to your room
the window was covered with a blanket and it was dark
it was like going to see the elephant man
you looked so tiny all wrapped up in a ball
        on your bed in your old room
you looked adorable with Pokémon sheets covering you
your sister told you i was here and you asked, "really?"
i could hear the surprise in your voice
although i do feel bad that i make you think
        i would leave you after this
i saw your face and it was swelled up beyond belief
your eyes were so swollen
        you could barely tell where they were
the lips that i've kissed many times
        were lopsided and purple
you had to peel your eyelids apart to see me
your hair was in thick clumps and matted down
there was blood in it still like on your shirt
the shirt you had on that night was new just like mine
yours hadn't even been washed
i could tell by the smell of it when i was holding you
your Boxcar Racer shirt was soaked in blood
just like my New Found Glory one
i looked at your swollen face
        and couldn't help but smile
because you still looked so beautiful to me
i'm gonna be there for you all through this
i went to the crash site after seeing you
the tire marks, kicked-up dirt, pressed-down weeds

i see now that we had to have flipped end over end
        as well as rolled
it must have been a sight
i estimate we went about 150 feet before stopping
i found a piece of a Good Charlotte sticker
        and a Yellowcard sticker
both of which still had glass
        from the window on them
i found a piece of the car that reads: 'warning
        to ensure safety be sure to fasten seat belt'
i found a squeeze bottle of lotion and some lipstick
        and one of your tapes
it still plays
one of the songs was a Linkin Park remix
that i assume was from the promo sampler
        i gave you
on the other side was the song "Everything" by Lifehouse
        that i have mentioned before
followed by "It's Been Awhile" and earlier is the song
        "Change" by Good Charlotte
i drove away with this tape playing
        and i got all choked up
everything looks different now
the day was bright but brighter than normal
i felt the wind on my skin
        and could smell more of nature around me
my parents voices and laughs
        sounded skewed but amazing
it all feels different after a near-life experience
most say near-death
but this has brought me closer to life than death
i called Marilyn and told her
        i wanted to see her and Will
it's time to take my life back
i need them in my life as much as you and i
        need each other
the world seems more beautiful after faced
        with the possibility of losing my life
and losing you
we will make it through this
and it is going to be a magnificent thing
just like you, my lovely

### road closed yesterday
  a thank you to Kelly

it has still only been a few days since we wrecked
and everything is so much better
i told you that i called Marilyn
and later on that night after i saw you
  i left a note on Will's car
i told him i loved him and that i need him in my life
he called me later on that night
  and he stopped by my house
i saw his eyes were red and he was very choked up
we talked for a few minutes
then he grabbed me and hugged me
  and cried into my shoulder
i had never seen him cry before then
i am kind of glad this was the first time
i cried too and we said we were sorry
i have never loved him so much
this has made me see that my life
  wasn't the way i wanted it
and that i had to fix it
you helped me save my friendship Kelly
you did me the biggest favor of my life
that car wreck was one of the greatest things
  that could have happened
it brought my past back to me
and it will bring me closer to you
thank you for everything beautiful
i'll see you in the future

## sparklegoat

let me take a moment please
to say to you the things that i love about you
i love how when you see me you feel better
and when i see you i feel sedated and content
when you touch me it is done with a nervousness
as if i'm an antique worth a fortune
and that you are so blessed to be doing so
when you kiss my cheek it sends chills
        through my entire body
how the small of your back and ass are sometimes
        slightly sweaty to the touch
        after you have been driving for awhile
in the back of Eric's car one night
        you put your head on my shoulder
        and the wind blew your hair all around
turning each strand into a whip that struck my face
        with a strange yet amazingly orgasmic touch
how headlights on cars would intermittently light up your face
and make your eyes glossy and shiny
        like two beautiful crystal balls
i love how when you hug me you melt into my body
i love knowing that we earned this
i love how i am the only one
        who can see the good in you
i love the good you put in me
i love being in you

i love you

## 10-8-02

she is beauty, elegance, sexuality
she represents everything magnificent in the world
you look into her and warmth fills you
her eyes meet yours and you melt into one
there is no tomorrow alone
only together for eternity
do not let her go for she is what makes you great

## october 17th, 2002 - thursday

rafters creak
children peak around the corner
his feet dangle from above
he ended it because of love
or rather a lack there of

———————————

hallways stretch before them
they grab the other's hand and kiss
look into each other's eyes and say their vows
at the end of the corridor is a light
a blazing fury to eternity
they walk into the brightness
and disappear into oblivion

## _____**transformation**_____

your tears twinkle in the moonlight
and i too can't help but cry
on the grass by ad astra pool we hug
i turn in my last kiss and say good-bye
you stand there shivering and shaking
        quivering and quaking
asking me why why why?
tears falling, knees locking, heart breaking
it's the night your dreams did die

i tell you i must be going
because you are never showing
the things i need to see
do you have trouble imagining
the way our life could be?
have you ever thought about growing?
you said you were all-knowing
but i guess you really don't know
anything about me

so that's the way it goes
my heart too much it shows
your love builds then dies then grows
it's truth no one ever knows
have you ever thought about growing?
you said you were all-knowing
but i guess you really don't know
anything about me

i call from another time-zone
to see how it goes today
i hear your cries through the phone
and yet you tell me you're "okay"?
i sleep and dream in a land unknown
now those feelings are said and shown
why wait 'til i'm 3,000 miles away?

have you ever thought about growing?
or have you finally grown too?
and now it's me who doesn't know
anything about you

## october 22nd, 2002 - tuesday

a child's brains drip on windowpanes
particles of memory splashed on a child's painting
a gun shell falls to the floor
a soul sent to for-nevermore
baby child's ear bleeds silence
in head resonates doomsday violence
swallow the pill of deception
a black smile confession
ended never forever gone
tomorrow now the burning sun
today he cried for god but made no difference
tonight only "extreme violence with no fixed point of reference"

---

there is no safety in our world
just hatred pure unfurled
darkness lies in jewels
pools of rotten fools
take a chance and dance
in a midnight death romance

## october 24th, 2002 - thursday

mass-produced pedophiles country condoned
pre-fetal terminations overblown
genocide mentality
date-rape actuality
dark-room-red reality
our children are on their own

---

dual back seat masturbation
midterm due date expiration

---

in the bathroom on a wet floor crying
last night in your bedroom
all your lies she was buying

## the uninvited

paralyzed by sanctions
fertilized by nations
in the gun fire cease
an infant cries for peace
mortified by terror
school boy turned pallbearer
father's life has been blown
died for a reason unknown
and they say it was all for the children
and they say it was all for the children
and they say it was all for the children
and they say it was all for the children
child-size gas masks
teen blood fills flasks
ship them off to a neverland
supposed to give a helping hand
to people who burn our flag
and they say it was all for the children
and they say it was all for the children

## a girl i once knew

garden gates in starlight
i wish i may i wish you might
forget what's been said and done
at least for this one night
go back with me to a time before
travel there, give me more
forgive me for everything Marilyn
i hurt you and don't know what for
in the past i see us golden
        don't walk away
in the past i see us golden
in the past i see us golden
in the past i see us golden

grant me a smile and then turn from me
in my mind i can see images of you and me
but it's over, i know that
be happy with him for eternity
live with him in apogee
so i won't have to see
no more you and me
forgotten sincerity
in my heart we spin in perigee
loving in equality
making love's duality
i need to forget you now
and it will come somehow
in the past i see us golden
        please walk away
in the past i see us golden
in the past i see us golden
in the past i see us golden

in the future i don't see anything

### october 28th, 2002 - monday

kiss the spider's children
engage asphyxiation
die da'daistic interpolation
no tears or cries for the martyr
Ian heard a red sky calling
watching the trees and leaves falling
never discovering mass salvation


### long dying forever

is it such a surprise
to see i'm your devil in disguise?
look into my eyes
i'm the cause of all your cries
and i just sit with muted sighs
you end our midnight trysts
and i cut my thinning wrists
i don't want to be without you
please i must insist
give us a few more nights
endure a few more fights
it's worth one more shot
give me all you've got
we have to say we tried


### november 8th, 2002 - friday

in a quick split-second decision
echo the sounds of Joy Division
take my heart and hold my hand
be my girl and i your man
strike a stance   make a stand
you are my only friend

october 2000 you said "i'm sure"
and together we were made unpure
making love to The Cure
enthralled and engrossed in 'Disintegration'
bodies touched and tickled with sensation
we will make it through tonight

## mareigner

black widows dangle from the treetops
and eclipse the burning sun
my wings expand and flutter
i raise my smoking gun
the man i seek confronts me
in his face i stick my rage
i'm speechless
but my thoughts are spoken
eloquently by my gauge




## autumn mystery*

the black ghost man leads you to the valley
your soul passing slowly through the trees
blood runs from your mouth
your body hanging from the gallows
townsfolk, women and children watch with ease

in your bed at night the voice told you
        to inform others
of ideas and thoughts that would seal your fate
there is no room for philosophy in these rustic times
the prophet's kids they burn, his wife they rape

the god that you pledged your life to
gives you thanks for what you did
in his paradise all will be behind you
you will be in his presence with your wife and kids

## november 20th, 2002 - wednesday

star-field children of the galaxy
dance in circles around the sun
yelling into the black hole
"this time of ours is done."

---

she cowers in an abandoned tenement
he looks at her bruised face
covering her naked body with her hands she shivers
he thanks the city for not tearing down this place

---

prairie, meadows, and farmland boys
cross-streets, cul-de-sacs, and posh-dog girls
longing for a change
wishing for a chance
trapped in a prefabricated time
forget their dreams and dance

---

twenty-five miles from the city
the field where they once laughed
fifteen years ago he remembers
he wants those days back

---

smell her skin and kiss her
taste her flesh and caress
give her everything you have to give
if not she will be gone before you have a chance

---

i'll die if i never have you
i'll cry if you leave me here
i'll not be able to forget you
after what you did though
i'll risk the pain

## a few words for Kelly on a saturday morning

i'm sorry i've not seen you
my sleep patterns are quite askew
all i've done is think about you
i've missed you so much, honey
have you missed me too?

you make me feel so great inside
and i can only think of one thing to do
i have something to tell you baby
hey sexy darling, beautiful gal
"i love you"

## december 8th, 2002 - sunday

"everything in my life is a story. and all stories are meant to be told. if i have the courage to admit the details of my life in writing, you should have the courage to endure the embarrassment and the pain of truth."

brett alan coker

## january 11th, 2003 - sunday

"the time in my life that i met her was a turbulent time. it was as if i was in an out of control river and needed to hold onto something. and it didn't matter what that something was, as long as it was stronger than me. and she was."

### nice car man, san diego!

fourteen years disappear
simply for a girl
at least you're happy
but i'm not
you're erasing me from your world

"can't wait 'til next tuesday"
something we always say
it's wednesday and it's a week away
and you are too far away to see
that i wait for you here
but there are no more tuesdays for me

i write about you in song and poem
and you don't seem to care
i want to hate you and forget our past
but i would never dare

i wish that i could say good-bye
but i have a lump in my throat
our friendship has faded and we cease to be
and it ended on a sour note


### end tomorrow cease

where is it that you went dear tripsy?
no one seems to know
oh i know where
to that guy's house
what's his name?
oh it's ...


### march 9th, 2003 - saturday

death came before me tonight
and left me with a sticky face
and didn't pay me my five bucks
the bastard

## gun mags, sunflower seeds & chlamydia

picture frames on doorsteps
imaginations run amuck
jabbering leper nations unchained
seven sciences, seven doors
        no one's sane
crescent moons on gravy trains
dreaming of a baby's smile
barreling silver bane
feasibility unheard of
        no chance monsignor
protagonist's antagonist is his mother
who smothered the child's face
tear stains of my shirt sleeve
blood on my shoes and hands
his eminence lay dying and saddened
at the entrance of his god's domain
troubled water transpires pyres
"pasted wings and foil rings do not an angel make"
yes they do
saraghina dance the rhumba
volpina dip my cock in your tea
third battalion retreats from the front-line
himmler eats human flesh
tasty, fishy, livid and gaunt
what is left of my mind?
where is my unicorn?
give me a dime with the fasci
control me with your ruse
mortal sins will not be deterrents
ethics all shot to hell
"asa nisi masa"
mother touch my nimble hand
adroit adolescents tell fairy tales
stories that bare no shame
sit on the shore of tomorrow
listen to the warmth of today
fantasize and harmonize for yesteryear
i'm failing to find my way

## eye steal neverland

our government is going to kill us
to begat the new world order
a plan conceived hundreds of years ago
no doubt that they'll achieve
control the oil and our funds will not be matched
politicians' pockets lined in hundreds
tycoons will strike their match
they buy the media and murder their foes
meanwhile we fuck each other
        and channel surf reality shows
they manufactured a.i.d.s. to destroy the unwanted
and bomb tenements in far-off lands
our guise is lending a sympathetic hand
soon our bodies will burn and our children will choke
all because of decisions by cunts in suits
who hate white trash, immigrants, niggers and fruits

oh, we pay for them to do this by the way


luckily i am white, not poor, educated and not gay
so i'll be the last to go
i'll starve in a nuclear winter
and dry up in a radioactive haze
at least i'll die before i have children
and thank heavens i have a gun
i will be able to take some of those
        "errand boys, sent by grocery clerks"
        with me
as i shoot up the national guard
their bodies will cover my yard
soon my country will kill me
and torture me with cyanide
        like they did the davidians
well that's fine i guess
i still have hell to look forward to

## a grand day out *

a long time has passed
and it's all the same
the same way you see
before you and me
before us and them
and never again
will we ever have anything to share
my love you won't bare
because you don't care
then again i don't either

i can't remember your smell
or the feel of your body in the dark
i promise our secrets i'll never tell
in my heart and body you left your mark
yet our tattooed life together is losing its color
as i've left and you love another

you're nothing i can touch anymore
a ripped-up picture on the bedroom floor
an e-mail on your birthday
there's not much left to say
a voice i can only hear in memories
no matter what happens it will never please
it will never again be like my senior year
when all intentions were clear
still our end was drawing near
and now you fading from my life
      is my greatest fear
but also the truest of reality
just go away from me
i don't want your pity
your face i hardly ever see

you're smearing pencil on
      an almost white again page
a tear-soaked letter wearing as thin as my hope
you're a fine wine growing sweeter with age
eventually i will be able to cope

you're the notes before a novel
      some things about you i cherish above all

a rushed cram before a test
    i hold on to the moments i love the best
a quick sketch before a final
    the sounds of our past aren't that clear
    but pop and skip like vinyl
you're a demo not a re-mastered track
    many of the bad things i did
    i wish i could take back

## allow me a minute ... *

we used to hang at the tower
a convoy of cars and trucks
farming the nearby grass
spitting from the very top
in this boy's mind his torment
apparently wouldn't stop

our golden memories sway with the wind
like his feet from the blackened beam
i wanted it to be my icon
and i never would have dreamed
a kid would end his time there
we would play some music, smoke a cigar
        or drink a beer

at the top you look around and all sounds fade away
and mix into white noise
at the top Will and i flew kites once
back when we were boys
i have spent many days here
with my family
my old dog codie
my friends
and many loves
i never once wrote my name on it with spray paint
although everyone does

all is forever
in your memory it waits
he climbed the stairs
which i have stepped upon many
        many times
he felt the breeze that has blown across my face

was it because of his parents?
or because of a girl?
how about a fear of tomorrow?
perhaps just the pain
seen in the world

Brianna sang there once
as i laid on my back

hypnotized
by the great expanse above
Kirk was there with me
and a tear
fell along my cheek

Tim, Derek and i smoked some cigars there one time
and we forgot to bring a lighter
so we sent Derek back down
to get one from his car
the time he was gone was extremely short
that is when we realized he could teleport

i took Marilyn there
within the first few weeks of us dating
back before we knew
we would end up this way
i clearly remember that day
i wonder what the kid would say
if he knew
that the place he stood
meant so much to so many
it was a refuge for those like me
in search of peace
i'd hope he wouldn't have done what he did
maybe he would have made a different choice

so much love in the world
so many good things
so many good people
so much friendship yet unused
i understand we could get the last two confused
but don't stop searching for it
it will come i promise
the light at the end of the tunnel
won't always be a train

i have been to the same dreary places
i have seen those decrepit parts of the mind
i have wanted my life to end
i thought once how you thought
i wanted it to stop
what i searched for i found

because i did not give up
i kept on
striven on       and won
and i'm saddened that you didn't
but you ended up this way because you quit

we used to hang at the tower
and now a new generation does
except when we hung out there
we never used a rope

## wm3

they're innocent you stupid fuckin' 'loids
how come you are so ashamed
        of your pitiful little cocks
that you make three innocent boys, now men
endure the hells of prison?
of deceptions and lies?
how the fuck can you look at your children
        and pretend to be a hero?
you are a bunch of cum-chugging re-re's
given the powers of the law to bring forth justice
but you fuck it up and ruin lives
then you go home
        and are laughed at behind your backs
you dumb jag-off'n nazis

## bogyman*

to rid the world of its pain
inflicting more is necessary
give me a gun and a hot-iron
to poke and prod and sear some flesh
then put a speeding ball of lead through each kneecap
one in the gut
one in the neck
singe the ears of tyrants with my poker
and then stick my barrell in their gut wound
and fire two rounds straight through
        their rotting flesh
i am nothing but fire
you can only fuel me with pain
throw me into any situation and many i will kill
try to douse me and i will merely flare up
something in my heart lets me know i am doing good
and my passion for death is pure
laugh at me but be afraid
all i live to do is kill you and your family
i am fire and death
to burn you and make you slowly die
torture every molecule
        of your brainwashed feeble mind
the fire in my eyes
lights the way for my darkness
i can fake my night time with lies
you can sleep and i will come
        and shine before you and engulf you
while you are awake i can make you
        see the blade of life
faking day for night
night in day
my flames will melt your heart
and i'll eat your crispy flesh

### march 17th, 2003 - monday

your lip gloss on my lips
and make-up on my shoulder


### school dazed

on my way to school today
i began to feel real gay
a bit of happiness filled my soul
as a bit of water seeped into
        a socky hole

when it rains everything glistens
and i can't help but feel sublime
ants will swim in puddles
        and worms crawl out to listen
to a little of the rain's pattering rhyme
yes, oh yes, i confess
it should rain all the time

i hope it rains so much, so much
that they'll close the school
no bus, no mess, no homework fuss
if i were principal i'd be one you could trust
        i would be no fool
i'd declare a rain day, like a snow day, how cool
hooray! hoorah! gooday! goodah!
yippee there is no school!

it's fun when it rains i tell you
some rules can be broke and bent
i want to play in the wetness
but now i must lament
i look down and i frown
        oh my!
        i am stepping in cement

## march 25th, 2003 - tuesday

daddy went to war
and i still don't know what for
he came home in a box
and upped a few stocks
at least "big oil" won't cry no more

———————

daddy said "freedom is a jewel."
and protesters called him a "fool."
fighting men supposedly bad
i, meanwhile, have no dad
mommy can't afford gas to get me to school

———————

my parents raised me right
we rarely had a fight
they sheltered me from sex and boys
and all those things that are bad
so i spent my time smoking hash
and threw many a drug-binge bash
i'm a 46-year-old virgin in rehab
i love you mom and dad


## quadnations

the story of yesterday.  i can't wait to see what happens.

———————

in a lifetime all you have to do is die

———————

highway overpass.  sleeping.  under the influence.

———————

diggity diggity
higgity cha!
miggity miggity
figgity da!
fuck you

———————

i think executions should be an olympic sport

———————

### star fruit and candy corn

your name is used in many songs
and it always sounds so right
i have something for you my dear that i wrote tonight
it has a beautiful melody, a simple rhyme and beat
when you hear it i hope it sounds so sweet

i'm sorry for our tortured past
never thought we would ever be
and never thought we'd last
we're not who we were
but i am finally sure
that you are her the one for me
to look and be and always see
you standing beside me

the future is not so clear
will we last a year?
our months as one
can never be undone
for we spent days together
and dreamt whether
the minute that we met
was our fate then set?
and as we fell in love
we grew into a life together
paved by wishes and dreams
graced by your stars above

"Kelly watch the stars"
and tell me what will be
as the angels hark
and step from the dark
asking "has anyone here seen Kelly?"

time still drags us further
along in the sands of time
all i have is you, my heart and yours
a pen, some love, a rhyme
it has been a while but it still feels short
yet our time as a couple will never feel too long
sitting beside you, smiling as The Movielife sang
"Kelly song"

this is my poem for you
set to a diddy, a tune
my love letter for you to make you smile
when we kiss again, in a short while
it will never be too soon

## pamela 36 take 1* (song)

september of '99
it became that time
when you didn't call
waiting for you in our home
crying in the hall
our bed is empty while you roam
i'm scared you're not, while i feel alone

is there a reason for this?
there has to be a purpose
tell me why you do this?
why you put me through this?

one week later, you're gone again
off to downtown and holding his hand
i cruise the bars not thinking ahead
      (looking for head)
gonna fill your empty, spot in our bed
you run off with boys, and leave me with girls
still we're together, what's wrong with this world?
we smile and chat, like nothing is wrong
we both want to leave, but neither is gone

is there a reason for this?
there has to be a purpose
tell me why we do this?
why we both go through this?
is it mere discretion or sheer indifference?

i'm looking at you
and i'm thinking of her
you're smiling at me
      but you're seeing his face
behind my back you touch
      behind your back we kiss
what is the point of all of this?
is it mere discretion or sheer indifference?

you say that you love me but i don't believe
i say it back, just to deceive
what we had is over, it has all been lost
now we're lying to ourselves

that we shared something once

i am tired of putting everything into
the nothing i get from you

is there a reason for this?
there has to be a purpose?
tell me why we do this?
why we both go through this?

is it mere discretion or sheer indifference?

## growing noah (song)

hello dear child i am your friend
take my hand i will carry you
through the light          into the end
don't be afraid of anyone, anything or dying
so much is ahead let's get going
you can be anything you want to be
just be yourself and you will see
the power you bare it is so great
so think ahead but live for today
through life and love you must blaze on
fight those wars that must be won
times will change and pain will come
but when all is said and done
you will see you're not alone
you are not the only one
your mom will cry and you will too
fail once or twice and dad'll look down on you
they have seen many things and you will too
faced many problems but came through
don't give up they have faith in you
tomorrow is not too far away
say whatever it is you want to say
do whatever you feel is true
follow your heart and mind too
be prepared cause adults do lie
they will tear you down but you must try
in life all you have to do is die
make the most of it and you'll see why
why we strive and why we fight
why we face each day and night
why we laugh and why we cry
why we live and why we die
why there's pain and why there's hate
why we work and why we date
why we fuck and why we share
why we love and why we care
religion, truth, and friends, and sex
the meaning of life you will never guess
someday my friend you will know
only when you learn and grow
make it through forever
                and reach the end of your show

### stumbling outta like (song)

if it's alright
i'm going to stay up and drink all night
write and then rewrite
our penciled past with permanent ink
and i may just stop and think
about what we had
and what we did
all we shared
and all things said
and the bad things i had done to you
and the reasons for why we are through

i know it's not supposed to be like this
but it's the way i've always been
crawling out of a hole i made
only to fall back in
i'll never be the man you want
just a failing friend
i promise i'll never do it
and i mean it when i say it
yet we both know it will happen again

i want it to be different just as much as you
you act like you don't believe me but i'll swear to you
i am gonna change someday just you wait and see
pick up your doubts
see this through
or i'll be the man you'll never see

## tripsy & the bandit

since '88 we have had a happy life together
elementary school recess, swing sets, vocab. tests,
      never knowing whether
it will last until we die
you have her now and i'm writing this
alone, drunk, and too stupid to cry
not brave enough to swallow my regret and dial
we both wait for the other's call
my guess is it will be awhile

throwing darts and billiard balls
a black camel 8 and a miller light cue
claymation movies, fire logs, and beta porn
and now nothing is all we do
softball teams and primal screams
dumping Kirk's desk on the classroom floor
smoking weed and stogies in the basement
sneaking in through the back door
golfing with cans of diet coke
falling off my bike when your peg hit my spokes
cruising high school nights away in the babe-layer
      and then eastbound and down
the t/a used to be your prize possession
      now it's all torn down
a lot of things are
now what do we have
is there anything you want to say?
i think it's a bad thing if you don't
and i am speechless too so far
you don't phone and i still never answer
i'd pick it up if i thought we had a chance or
perhaps if i forget my pride

the nights get dark and mosey will bark
you at your house and me at mine
as we stare up at the same moon
seeing all the universe
remembering all that's been done
forgetting all that's gone
wanting to be forever
wishing to always be young
or at least to shine and share one more moment

a funny story or two
but i lost all hope
when she left me and found you
when you took her hand and your love began
she threw our time as one on the pyre
you gained all i had of her
while she stole everything of you from me
i lost you won
she won i lost
my consolation prize was a handful of anguish
and it is fueling my raging fire

fourteen years have passed now
having always seen your face
spending our teenage years drinking
and wasting away at your place
how did we come this far?
i never thought between us
anything could or would go wrong
i see no future
it is all behind us now
we are ending ...
      ... like this song

i never said "good-bye"
and too scared to say "hello"
i hope you know i love you
and i miss you so
all things fade
this is the finale ...

## forever

all our time together feeling so important
making love on your bed
       blaring Something Corporate



## troy's bucket* (song)
unfinished

good-bye to my family
so long my loved ones
my childhood has ended now
all i had is gone

———————

what happens on the road ahead
you can never tell
i'm looking back and dreaming of
my 21 wishing well

———————

in a land of ivory bullets
with sparkling chromium shells
i'm lost and being found
still searching for my 21 wishing well

## mastorna* (song)
unfinished

a band i'll never sing in
a song we'll never play
poetry, prose, and pictures
never seeing the light of day

_____

a novella never finished
i always get discouraged

_____

all things left behind
born in my mind and forgotten
these are all signs of the time
now we give up and in
and never begin
what we set out to do
they end before begin
are over before they're through
"plan your work, and work your plan"
keep thinking and repeating little train
"i think i can, i think i can"

_____

follow all thoughts through until completion
no great idea deserves deletion

### swatch dogs & diet coke heads* (song)
unfinished

you are being lied to, everything you know is wrong
burn you cell phone, crash your suv,
    stop listening to creed
put on some Coltrane, Steel Train
    and pick up a book
some Rollins or Selby will do
there is a whole world of allusion and fantasy
illusion and reality
out there, and it's all for you

rip the names off your clothes
find all of your foes
they are the ones who take your money
and sell you worthless dreams
you're not a walking billboard
drugs and not sex is absurd


### may 21st, 2003 - wednesday
why would you never envision
the beauty that could have been shared
    by you and me
i don't doubt a dazzling bride you'd make
to a husband who could actually stand you


### may 26th, 2003 - monday
Coltrane's music is like sex without any physical contact.  the emotion is there and the passion and the love.  the sensations and thrills of an orgasm but no fumbly, sticky groping to destroy the mood.  it is atmospheric and mystical.  it is divine.  it is impulse.

## anthem

okay, so here's the thing. skinny people can not help being skinny as much as fat people can't help being fat. it is the way we were made. our metabolism and body structure and all of that. i was a fat fuckin' baby. i was 10 lb. 11 oz. at birth. and now at the age of 21 and 6'1" tall i am extremely under weight for my height. a friend of mine who is shorter than me weighs ten pounds more than i do. and i know another guy who is as tall, if not taller than me who weighs 127 lb., to my 143 lb.

    people who are heavier are always giving us shit, saying "oh, i hate you, you're so skinny." "god, i wish i was as skinny as you, i'm so fat." fuck that. when you tell a person, "gosh, you are so skinny!" it is like me going up to a fat person and saying "god damn you're fat." skinny people, skinny white guys mainly, since that is what i am and the only group i can speak for, are just as self-conscious about being skinny as fat people are about being fat. i wish i could put on ten or more pounds as much as fat people want to lose ten or more pounds. i eat, just so you know. i eat a fuckin' lot, but you know what? it doesn't change a thing. and if i work out all i get is tone, i don't get buff. so here again i am a 21-year-old who is 6'1" and weighs 143 lbs. who has arms like sticks and legs like, well, longer sticks. it's not very threatening. i'm not weak by any means, but to look at me you'd think i was a wuss. i can fight and have but i will never be able to scare anyone off by using my bulging biceps or throbbing forearms.

    my girlfriend is about a foot shorter than me so i am very insecure about that because it has to look really funny when we hug, because it looks like i am hugging a little cousin or some little kid. i have a bony pelvis that i'm sure doesn't feel good when making love, and i have no ass whatsoever. seriously, it just goes from my spinal column straight down to my legs. there is nothing in-between.

    so please keep in mind that we, the skinny white men of america, do not like our weight to be brought up. if i were to go to the fat white men of america's convention and yell, "hey, you guys are so fat i hate you" i'd get pelted with a lot of rib sandwiches. actually they'd probably eat those and throw all of the vegetables and healthy foods at me.

    i am a skinny white man who will always be skinny and will always be persecuted because people assume that i am happy with my weight. i am not happy with it. but i do accept it. so if you are fat, accept it and you'll be happier. if i could gain ten pounds that would be cool. but i am content with what i am as long as you fatties shut the fuck up!

## tony watch your head*

"since september 11th ..."

  " ... post 9/11 environment ... "

"in the wake of september 11th ... "

  " ... aftermath of 9/11 ... "

"as we saw after september 11th ... "

  "september 11th and beyond ... "

supposedly we didn't see it coming.
and that it is a horrible tragedy.
it is. or was.
can we move on yet?

what about oklahoma city?
what about ruby ridge?
what about the 3,000 dead in panama?
what about the extermination, third-reich style,
  of the davidians at carmel in waco?
what about the hate bred and unleashed at columbine?
jonesboro?
hiroshima?
nagasaki?
somalia?

what about the kid whose mom is at work and daddy overseas? all he has is his music, a poster of someone he'll never meet on his wall, and a video game where you drive around and kill people. a television that displays car crashes, people who'll eat their own hair and swim in feces for money?

what about the girl whose dad used to touch her while mom said nothing. then dad went back to the church to preach and mom went to the bar. the girl cried and then shot up. she was pregnant at 13.

and the child who will never meet his dad because he was killed while occupying a country that is no longer a threat.

the boy whose mom left him because she won the lottery, got her breasts enlarged, tummy tucked and her face laser resurfaced. so she was young and beautiful looking again so she road off with the first guy she met. and dad was too busy working two jobs to stop her. is it his problem he can't get it up anymore after breathing all of the fumes and toxins in our air and at the plant he works at. drinking down arsenic and smoking cancer.

i believe america is a spoiled child. america was raised by an abusive parent and then ran away. we got a credit card and a free place to stay. once we killed all of the brown people. we used that credit card to buy the biggest gun so we had all of the power. but we were never trained to hold that power. we hide behind pride and honor. pride for killing and degrading minorities and honor of raising pedophiles and rapists.
we are that kid in your class who never paid attention and always acted out. no cause to fight for but would fight anyway. you insult us and we'll kill you and call it justice. we'll murder your people because they are of a different religion, or have dark skin and don't have money. we are a bastard child who is left the house for the weekend and invites over their rich friends to play. plenty of booze, drugs and sex. but outside we are all clean-cut, god-fearing, mainly judeo-christian, taxpaying, helping hand lenders.

we punch, and kick and bite and stab and kill and shoot and rape. and when we skin our knee we look down and cry and don't understand what we are feeling. "pain? loss? what are these? i shouldn't be able to get hurt because i watch television. i listen to j. lo, and watch american idol! oh, that simon is so mean! i wonder who Joe millionaire is going to pick? i don't get it? people don't die when we go to war. they just fall down and lie real still. and all that blood on the ground will eventually be soaked back up by their bodies and they will be okay. i don't get it? no, you don't get it! those people who die over there are not humans. they are savages who eat rice and bread and never bathe and worship an evil lord and speak all weird and it's okay that we kill them because we are doing good. a war is just a television story? it's all fake."

"okay here is what we are gonna do. i am going to invade your land. kill your people, rape your women, suck up your natural resources, put in a fast food chain that you will get paid less than our white workers at. we will take over your homes and give them to our workers and put up a large asbestos-filled tenement for you and your thirty family members. you have to read this bible and this bible only. and you have to speak english. i know we're not in america but that is what we speak so you have to conform to us. okay? and no talking back because we don't listen to squabbling by the help. oh, and all of that love you make because sex is natural and okay, well you can't do that anymore. you are sinners if you do that. here, have some heroin and cocaine and raise your kids to abuse this stuff and they will never touch each other in the naughty places."

i am gonna stop writing now. i am too depressed because i know i am right.

## lampkin lane * (song)
unfinished

we have made the decision
tonight is the night
i want it to be special
it will feel so right
    go slow

## coffee mugs, ninja turtles & light sabers (song)
unfinished

remember that song from when i was a kid
you quoted it when i was in trouble
this is what you said
"everything i do, i do for you"
but now what do you do for me
why won't you see what i have inside
and all the good things i will be
i will be something great and then you'll care
when it's all too late

___

i never had any emotional support
you tore it all down
like a living room fort

___

why won't you believe in me?

## june 30th, 2003 - monday
"it's not that i don't love right now.
i just never stopped loving back then."

## _____**pop tart body shot**_____
atavistic decadence
shot full deep-fried
turbulent evanescence
hot plate, drip-dried
through the walls
her cumming screams cry
he pounds and she tears up
but smiles a cheshire smile
telltale makers of thought
and beatific voice
choices of choice
to choose or lose a war
the man who stands in the doorway
      of his childhood's room
has long phallic phangs
which glow and shine
      like cum in ultraviolet light

precognitive erected whores
go down on each other between johns
the salty shot slides
down there esophageal path
to join its regiment of soldiers
      in an acidic plunge

like a boy who finds his father's gun
or a girl touching her clit for the first time
danger is ahead
two loads are gonna be blown
into the air as it cuts lines
      through the white-noise lies
      of our nation

tell me about the ghettos
about the syringe-filled ponds
and condom-overloaded septic tanks
everyone gets the injection
      one way or another
vaseline eyes make the world easier to see
or easier to accept and understand
there is no tearing or anal leakage

oak tree branch snaps
awakening my pure consciousness
Carroll strokes my head and puts me back to sleep
he then nods off himself
on a mainline shot
Ginsberg sits on the window sill
licking his lips as he watches
       the boys on the streets
young blacks playing street ball
all of their rage already in place
       not yet unleashed
Kerouac lays out his mat
in the southwest corner of the loft
he repeats a forgotten mantra
sips some wine and speaks to us
about unchained mechanics
and ephemeral loves
sacrilegious texts
derelict closet cases


across the street a bold-faced liar
       with the nose of a sharpei
tells his children to obey the computers
to drink their sodas
eat their fast food
and be home in time for the sitcoms and reality shows
instructing them to avoid trees
all forms of nature
books
open minds
and curiosity
the only cat it didn't kill
       was a boppin' hep


hark to speed-freak latinos
to shut the blinds
on their way out to see the transcendence
       of mohammed
to check up on the beats who lounge at 81st
smoking liggetts and drinking cap'n
tell those lazy-ass crackas
to check up on the cunts
       on renner rd.

who screw by a clock
        set to a scream
pop "ups" and then fuck
        listening to Air

wherever the pen goes
my hand is soon to follow
where my hand goes my cock
        is sure to be
17 and fucking a stranger
battering her with my drumstick
and basting her bags
        with my flow
in the mirror there is a face
i no longer remember
with a mind that is corrupting
all those around
the pleading nymphettes
        and drooling queers
all is coming to an end
all is going to conclude
all is coming to an end

## the lot *

you can laugh at my emotions
       and mock my art
but when i stand at the doorway of glory
you will still be going to keggars
       with trust-fund babies
       and date-rapists


## potion of oblivion *

you set my heart ablaze
and i burn so bright
i see through you
and view your beauty
you are my celluloid dream

## soledad st.* (song)
### written with Franklin Keith Richard Cline

it started to rain as we walked on
on through the night, into the darkness
holding hands, connecting eyes
passing a window i've seen a thousand times
but tonight it's different 'cause i'm with you
it's an interesting feeling
re-falling in love
i never thought we'd be back here again

the rain stops for a moment
then begins anew
just like we could
and this millionth kiss
feels like a first

wasn't sure if you needed my help
to fix your bad day
but i was there anyway
my car broke down a mile from your house
then we were all alone
footsteps falling on concrete
not as loud as they used to be
the angelic hum of a streetlight reminds me of you
if only for a moment

it started to rain as i walked on
on through the night, into the darkness
trembling hands weeping eyes
passing a window i've seen a thousand times
missing what i saw before
like always it's without you

### july 24th, 2003 - thursday

i am 21. almost 22. and i don't like to revert back to who i was. i am not a child anymore. i am not a teenager. i don't enjoy running around skate parks and goofing off because i am too old for that. it's not that i think i am better than anybody else i just want to progress and be better than what i am.

### july 24th, 2003 - thursday
untitled and unfinished

the song said tuesday's gone
and you never did believe

burn away our childhood dreams
and adolescent fears
destroy forgotten hopes
to relive teenage years

---

drown out your sorrow
throughout teenage years
take a trip through reality
surpass adolescent fears
put on 'Smokey & the Bandit'
and toss me another beer
we don't know it yet
but soon i won't be here

## because of moments like this
      for Kelly

five years is not so far apart
    when i pledge you my life
    and you give me your heart
the longer you are by my side
    it is plain to see
that i am growing further
    from being that supposed man
    that you know i used to be

send me a letter
    sealed with a kiss
    and stained with a tear
wrap it in a ribbon
    pulled from your hair
spray it with the perfume i bought you
    and set it on the floor
close your eyes and listen to your heartbeat
    i'm just outside your door
hold my hand and let's go out
    and lie beneath the moon
    we do this every week
    but tonight will change everything

because the stars will look at you

they'll see your smile
    smell your scent
and it will remind them
    why they shine

like me they want to spend forever
    in your arms
    and on your mind

### return to me *

what do you look like now?
what have you become?
i hear stories about you
and what i hear is a person
who is nothing like what i remember

i'm running out of things to say
        and write about you
i am forgetting all of the things we once did

as you know i watch a lot of movies
and whenever i watch a good romance movie
        where the guy is so sweet and amazing
i always think of who you once were
somehow i feel like that's not you now

it's 4:55 in the morning
i've had a few glasses of wine
my mind is flooded with thoughts of you

i have began many things in my life
        too many i have yet to complete
but i can never be whole again
        until we fix what we caused

all i can say
is that i still miss you

## 1549

i will never know all there is to know
but i will not give up trying
through all of this i will continue
    my search for truth
and i will always strive to understand
i believe that creation comes from destruction
much like order out of chaos
and light from darkness
before you can build something
    on a strong foundation
you have to rip up the ground and remold it
and pour on fresh cement
fresh ideas and feelings
over the years i have torn myself apart
i have put myself in many places
    and fought my way out
jumped naked into the deep-end
    and struggled to stay afloat
as i look into the future
i can predict more trials and tribulations
more pain, conflict, tough times
but love and good times as well
i will fail many more times
yet i also will succeed
    in those places where i have failed before
through my writings i have seen who i am
and i can understand why i do some things i do
i condescend to a lot of people
    to make myself feel smart
i flaunt a lot of the things i have
because for some reason
    i am proud of a lot of possessions
i talk to people very often in a tone
    that says to them i am better than them
and that no one has seen the things i have
    and i am more worldly
we all know this is false
the truth is i am still a child
    inside this new man's body
i still can not support myself
    or maintain financial stability
but i am fully aware of this and continue to try

i am scared of all of the wrongs
        i have committed to others
and ashamed of things i have said
        and things i have written
but i continue on
i am no different than anybody else
i am the same
i am not special by any means
i am just me
one of 6 billion pieces of crap
        i just pretend to be unique
what have i seen these last few years?
what have i learned?
i lost the woman i spent two years of my life with
my first real love and relationship
i drove her away by my childish and selfish actions
i treated the one who i now love like crap
because i placed the blame on her
i didn't take responsibility for what i did
and i tried to hate her while loving her in secret
i wallowed in self-pity
        and wanted everyone to feel sorry for me
i lost my best friend
well he lost me
it could have been saved
        but neither gave in to what is right
we just sat back and waited
        and it ended before we knew
i attempted to make something more of myself
        by going to college
but reverted back to my elitist mentality
        and said i didn't need school
when the truth is i couldn't hack it
        and didn't want to put forth energy
i was in a car wreck which could
        have claimed my life
but instead it opened my eyes
        to love that was right before them
and i've never been happier
        so that's good
i have become a lot smarter due to my reading habits
but even there i could improve
        by trying to understand the books being read

as opposed to just trying to read as many as i can
    just to say i did
my family basically ended
    although it just changed
my parents divorced
and the way i lived my life for 20 years has changed
it feels like yesterday i was 18
and the day before that i was 10
i got myself into debt and am still slowly
    crawling out of that hole
i still have not accomplished
    too much since high school
there are many things yet undone
    and unlearned
    and not quite understood

looking into the future once more
    here is what i see
i will leave the house i have lived in since 1984
leave the neighborhood and memories
maybe even get my own place with a friend
perhaps my job will change
a new friend will come
an old friend will leave
that one who is gone already
    will grow even more distant
that girl i loved will be a blurry image
    and weak voice in my head
the girl i love now may squeeze me tighter
or open her arms and release me
her love for me may fade
or mine for her
i hope not though

many of these things frighten me
many make me feel warm and fill me with hope
still i feel something dark ahead
    death
    or pain
mine or someone else's
no matter what i will hit it all head-on
i do see that i have matured
i do see i am making progress

i do see i can be more in my life
i do see a happy ending
i understand that just because i fall
        doesn't mean i can't climb back up
i understand that just because i cry
        doesn't mean i will always miss what i lose
i understand that soon my life will change more
        in good ways and bad
i understand that i am the creator of my own world
i understand i am responsible for
        the way my life goes
i understand i am somebody
i understand tomorrow will be okay
i understand that all the days
        that came before me served a purpose
i understand that while i study and analyze the past
        the future passes me by

i understand that i am a tall, skinny, kind of attractive, somewhat funny, slightly intellectual, white suburban male who drinks too much soda, has bad teeth, a yellow toe, some pimples on his back, is bad at listening and is pretentious, egotistical, conceited and arrogant, has an affinity for younger girls, a penchant for sex, who masturbates too much, never acts as much as he talks, thinks he is better than others, sometimes two-faced, sometimes lies, slightly racist but tries not to be, lazy, self-centered, mooching, but still very giving, neurotic, self-serving, depressed, occasionally a false bourgeois, full of delusions of grandeur, quits a lot of things before he finishes, lives in his mind, tries to be what he is not, is embarrassed by who he is and things he does, a cheat, a womanizer, a user, a cynic, a pessimist, a bad friend, a rebel, an outsider, a piece of shit, and a fucking fake, of an elitist mentality, makes fun of people who live their lives the way he wishes he would let himself live, horrified of change ...
    ... yet ...
        ... i will face the coming days with full knowledge of my faults and of my strengths and that my work is not finished and my life still has to be lived ...
        ... i will wake up tomorrow and read this and know what i am and who i am ...

        ... and for now that is all i need to understand.

## ... added bonus ...

the following piece as you will read was written back in 2001. i had a dream one night that fucked my head up so bad that i was nauseous all day at work and depressed for a week. a week later i sat in my dark basement with a candle burning and over the period of an hour i wrote what follows. it is the best description of any dream that i have ever written. i will include it in my book of dreams called <u>fleeting glimpse</u> but felt it deserved to be in here due to its somewhat eerie predictions. this dream is extremely prophetic. it foreshadowed something that would eventually play itself out in my life and in my work in <u>understanding thursday</u>. it was the first piece written in a series of pieces that chronicle the slow decrescendo/denouement and destruction of a friendship. this dream told me of something that would come to pass a year later. (although not based on a dream the poem "clockwork pupils" written on december 5th, 2001 became reality on december 14th, 2001)

it is a very strenuous read due to the format in which it was written but with the exception of fixing typographical errors this is a completely virginal work. i just sat there and let the dream play and play in my mind and i was consumed by the pain i felt and just let the emotions do the typing for me. any structure was lost. i had no idea what it looked like as i wrote i just wrote and wrote. stopping only to have large and hard outbursts of sobbing. taking breaks to try and breathe and wipe the tears from my eyes. this piece still makes me tear up. this piece scares me because of the things that came after it. i do fear that it will all come true.

     and i hate it for that

# ... a dream for lamentation ...

may 24th, 2001, 1:10 a.m. - 2:25 a.m.

it's one thirty in the morning
and i am alone
alone in my basement and it is one thirty
                and i hurt
something has grown inside me that has changed me and made me
feel pain that i've not felt before
and i must confess this
hopefully to appease it        but it won't        i   k n o w
this

i am to confess a dream  a vision i dreamt
in a dream              it was about my friend
                           Will        and it made me
hurt
even though it was not real

           it killed me inside and i feel it still        i
hate myself and i want to die for what i've done
but not even what i've done but did        but not even that—
what i dreamt i did

           but it's all the same
this vision was telling me something and i respect that and thank
that            but fuck that vision     i fucking hate you
my mind          it caused this        or did i?
but aren't we one?      my mind and me?

           but i still hurt and need to confess
what i've dreamt i've done
        but not even that        what i'll do


and the confession of this dream/vision/pain begins ...

it was a grey day        a winter day and it was grey or
gray and cold        it was in the country on a grey winter day
     gray

there were clouds in the sky     the grey/gray sky
but not too many of these gre/ay puffs

they were dreary as one might expect and the wind blew ever so slowly         but briskly and cold         it was cold and grey         gray and cold

walking         i was walking through the country         a foot of snow on the ground         the best kind of snow if there is such a thing         the good packing snow and it was also grey

did i mention i dream in monochromatic gray?... grey?

so everything was a hint of grey/gray

i stumbled as i walked ... partly from my worn sneakers in the snow         mostly from the blurred vision due to inebriation         i knew where i was going but not exactly         i knew where i was going but wasn't sure if it was the right place
the place i needed/ wanted to be


the house comes into my sight         popping into view out of nowhere or so it seemed to me at least         a m o d e r n   d a y house but with an old ancient feel         it was grey         w i t h   a gray roof         with a grey chimney and gray snow surrounding a majority of the house         o r         m o r e specifically the yard was a fence

it was grey         but in color dreams/visions it would be brown         it was made of wooden beams         b u t   y o u know if the beams were as old as they seemed they may have been weathered and actually been grey         gray like the chimney
the house         the snow         and the sky         and me inside

i climbed         no         toppled over the fence laughing a jilted jumbly drunken         asshole of a laugh and continued on


my grey shoes leaving gray prints

in the front yard now i start to question myself         is  this
where i am supposed to be?            is this where i was headed?
        it is the right address but is it his house?


i reach the porch              it hadn't been shoveled clear of the
grey snow


the doorbell is rung       then i retract my white brittle hand
which felt as if all of the blood in it had frozen          w h e n    i
contracted my hand the joints and veins felt like piano wire
they were hard and the tension was making them tear
soon they would snap
            we all eventually do


as i wait for an answer i nervously shift my weight back and forth on
my feet        mashing the grey snow           into a watery gray
slush         i cross my eyes to look at my nose
red, not surprising


even though i dream in monochromatic gray i can tell me nose is red
        or would be the equal of red had this been real

                or when it becomes real

my ears burn from the wind constantly blowing on them
my nose runs and i'm too careless to sniff the mucous back up


              i check my watch            barely able to see
that it is ten fourteen in the evening        or it could be
morning                my eyes were so watery it was tough to tell
          and i was drunk



                a commotion is heard from within
my tension is heightened       i wait to see if i am at the right
place


the door opens       it is not who i expect          but i am
not completely wrong

the young brunette looks familiar				as if i know her
but i don't think i do			but i someday will
	or so i fear

i suck in a mouthful of air				the coldness running into
my mouth and lungs

	is Will here?
the young girl looks at me as if she knew me or maybe will someday
	yes he is, come on in.

stepping into the house the instant warmth was so refreshing and
invigorating			but i knew inside that eventually i will have
to deal with the burning		the burning of your senses
your hands and feet and nose and ears		as they adjust
from the			deadly cold			to the hellish heat

the house feels comfortable		it feels like home
but it's not		not  mine at least			will it be?

i scan the room with my blurry watery eyes			the young
brunette wanders off to find the person i requested
Will

i feel safe		i am proud i found his house
looking around i know it's his house		built with his
hands		his strength and his warm gentle heart		i t
had been so long and i missed his glow and the look of his eyes when
he finished something		his talent

	my mind wanders for a moment		b e f o r e	m y
attention is caught by a presence

the brunette has returned		i now feel as if she is his
wife		maybe too young

	here he is. she says to me

i turn and see him		the one i came to see and have
missed so much		it had been forever		ten years
maybe fifteen		maybe not that long			m a y b e
longer

i turn and see the boy i grew up with      rode bikes with            a
kid who shared almost all of my childhood memories a guy i've loved
like no other     a guy who is one of a kind who i cherish so much
who i could never be without          i see him         i ' v e
missed him so       and now i see him           god it is so
great to be in his house that he built with his love and heart
and i've missed him          and i see him


                        it was Will


but it wasn't who i remembered       it's not the Will i knew
not the guy i spent my years playing in the creek (crick) with
standing on our handle-bars with      skateboarding with
this was not the Will i knew          and cherished          i t
was not the Will i remembered or missed


            but it was the Will i came to see

he walked slowly into the room not looking up         but down
at his feet   shuffling only inches at a time like an old man
an old man who had done many things with his life
seen so much       and had so much         as if he'd
worked everyday all day of his life        he was brittle like
my shivering hands         and this was Will
my Will       the Will i came to see       but not the one i
cherished and missed but it was him       Will


            he didn't just look old and worn and tired and fed up
with life and the world and everyone in it      no he didn't look
like it             he was it          the old man
this was Will    he was old      and tired and worn     this was
Will who had done so much and seen so many things and achieved so
much and had a great life        but looked on the verge of
death        sick of everything        this was Will
who appeared as if he'd done nothing       achieved nothing
        but also wanted nothing     this was that Will
but not the bike riding guitar playing Will
            not my Will    the one i came to see           t o
rejoice with          about our teenage years        drinking

partying          speeding in our cars          causing a ruckus
          being young          this was not that Will          he
wasn't young          he was the old man i saw          t h e   o l d
man i saw he was          and i became sad
but i blew it off



my arrogantness kicked into gear and my mouth switched to on
and away i went

          hey Will you son of a bitch how you be man? so long          it
has been so long, hasn't it Will
my best friend in the world? man its good— have you lost weight—
you look great. so what's going on my best buddy?
inside i know what will happen


Will says nothing          he cares no more about the
world          or the people in it          or his life
he just wants to be alone and remembered what he achieved


or so i thought          and i was
wrong



next we are sitting on the wooden floor eating dinner
no longer just the three of us          there are two more people
with us          although i only saw one i felt the other's presence
by the fire ... eating on the floor was Will, Tim, and Kirk
Tim i saw          Kirk i could feel was there
and they ate by the fire          by the fire they were eating
and laughing and having a good time          ten feet away
(felt like miles)          i sat on the floor eating   almost alone
but not really          the young brunette was there
and we talked but no words were said

she was not his wife i could sense that now but a daughter or a
caretaker or both          both it was

               as we chatted without words i realized something
and it was that realization that killed me inside
Will did not hate the world              he                    wasn't
sick of the people or of living he hadn't changed it was me
Tim and Kirk and Will        none of them were changed it was
me

i came there expecting a red carpet gala        to be patted on the
back and told congratulations           but i didn't deserve it

i knew that i had left them          Will     Kirk    and Tim
        i left them behind     without caring and i know that and
i ...

        i no longer knew them    who they were   or what they liked
or what they were like                    i didn't know the
Will that i came to see to rejoice of the harmonious past i didn't know
him


          come to find out i was not alone        his daughter knew
him not as well         she had her own life              Will was
never there         always working earning a living
slowly dying        Will was old now          older than  Kirk
and Tim      and older than i       but we were all the same
age last time i looked


last time i looked we were also best friends              i  g u e s s
that changed with Will's age

his daughter had her own things her own life          i  f o u n d
myself intrigued by her but falsely       i knew
no      i felt   that i was hitting on her          t a l k i n g  to her
because i wanted to fuck her          just nod my head and say
yes yes that's interesting        anything for Will's daughter to fuck
me              Will changed    he was older          T   i   m
changed with Will but not older but different        K   i   r   k
changed

                              i was the same pathetic fucking
child            and i wanted to die                and soon i
did


next     i was hugging Will           he was in my arms and i
could feel him breath          i could feel his age through his skin
          i could sense his emotions          i grabbed him tight
and hugged him and told him i missed him and that i was sorry for
leaving


                i left them behind            i threw them away
Tim            and Kirk           i threw them away
left them behind for what        i don't know              i t
doesn't matter          i'm so sorry i left you and our past
and i left you and i can't believe i did and i should die


                i can't believe how i could do this and i left and you
hurt          i hurt you          i hurt you all
and i can't believe i did this and i'm so sorry you were hurt and i am
so sorry


                Will inhales deeply and lets out a muted sigh and i
felt it         the lack of care            he doesn't care
how i feel or how sorry i am all he cares about is that i tossed them
away         he looks at me as if i were a stranger


                and i was           am           will be

and he says

          cancer            that's what he says
cancer

i am going to die


and he tells me this and i start to cry i cry as he tells me this
       my best friend is going to die my best friend of thirteen years
forty three by Will's age       and he has cancer and he will die
and i left him and the others       and they don't care about
me       and he will die


Will    walks away       as i am bombarded with every bad
emotion    tormented       for my best friend Will he
will die    i left him       tossed him away
and he doesn't care       he will die and leave me like i left
him and he doesn't care       he is glad that i hurt    i
should hurt for leaving them       leaving behind my best
friend Will    who once played in the creek with me
and rode bikes with me on a warm summer day    Will who i
came to visit to rejoice and talk of the past    and he is
glad i am crying for i deserve to hurt    for him hurting    my best
friend Will wants me to hurt    because he hurts


       and he will die       he will die knowing that i
left him    and that he hated me for doing so and he was happy
that i was hurt and crying he will die    Will my friend
bikes    creek    summer    he will die
not the Will i knew    not the Will that i came to see
not the Will that could build a house    not the Will that i
knew who could fix any car    and that loved me like a
brother    this is not that Will
Will ...


not the Will i loved       i loved him
and i left him behind and i hurt and he will die and he is glad    he
will die leaving me like i did him    he wants me to cry and feel pain
       he will die and i will cry

this is not the Will who was my best friend          who had
the grey house          with the gray snow in his yard
this is not that Will          but it is the Will ...

                                        ... that will die

                    hating me












p.s. as i conclude this book now, as i write this, september 15th, 2003, i have not seen Will in 9 months. he does not have cancer or anything like that. but he and i are no longer best friends, or so it feels. i met him back in 1988 and fourteen years later, december 29th, 2002 was the last time i ever saw him...

... i am sure i will see him again someday ...

... i just hope i know him when i see him.

## *2018 Notes*

*'til the streetlights came on* is where it all started; and *ars gratia artis* is where I believe I truly found my voice: my own personal style of writing.
*understanding thursday* is the shitty bridge between the two.
I dislike this book the most out of everything I have written.
In *'til the streetlights came on* I was naive and didn't know better.
In *understanding thursday* I was naive, but thought I knew better than I did.
This book is extremely disjointed and all over the place.

If I went back through and cleaned out all the stuff I didn't like, this book would be close to blank. Not to say that there isn't some good stuff in here. But not good in the great sense, but good in the sense that a lot of key moments in my life were caught as they happened.
The stuff with Will and Marilyn, and the beginning of Kelly and I.
And especially the car wreck.

*understanding thursday* paved the way for all the stories that would come in *ars gratia artis* and beyond. And if you overlay this book with the events of my life; this is the book that begins to document the quasi-end of the closeness I once had with childhood friends. The Lenexa Brothers began to fade and my life focused more on the Regal Crew and Kelly.

It's much like my first real journal *The Tuesday Journals: Year 17 - Untitled*, (which technically predates *The Tuesday Journals*) it's not written well at all; but key moments and dates are documented.
And it its own way that's more important.

**the*BAC***
2018
*West Plaza*
*Kansas City, Missouri*

## Series One     (1998 to 2006)

'til the streetlights came on
understanding thursday
ars gratia artis
... for the minutes ...
in lucem proferre ...
... de nocte
x-rated
corruptio optimi pessima
reality vs. perception

## Series Two     (2007)

White Lies & the Confusion of Day Dreams
Black Truth & the Comprehension of Nightmares
Gray Days & the Possibility of Loveless Eyes
Golden Dust & the Resurgence of Youthful Trysts
Magenta Scars & the Delusions of Erudite Whores
Violet Dust & the Detriment of Broken Homes
Green Dreams & the Overflow of Orchidaceous Nights
Silver Rays & the Revolution of Dystopic Cliques
Cyan Lines & the Metamorphosis of Cyclical Tales

## Series Three     (2008 to 2012)

Junkyard Robot
In A World Of Reverse
A Treatise On Repose ...
See The Whole Board
Hums In Hollow Heads
270 Days Later
402 Roosevelt
24 Highway
10-14

## Collections - Selected

iJihad
iKnew
iZobot
iFade

## Collections - Complete

3,002 Days
Of An Example Made
Mind Shards
Fiber Scars

www.ingramcontent.com/pod-product-compliance
Lightning Source LLC
Chambersburg PA
CBHW051931160426
43198CB00012B/2103